D1384927

A
LESSON
OF
LOVE

The Revelations
of
Julian of Norwich

Edited and Translated
for Devotional Use
by Father John-Julian, O.J.N.

Walker and Company
New York

First published in the United States of America in 1988 by the Walker Publishing Company, Inc.

Published simultaneously in Canada by Thomas Allen & Son Canada, Limited, Markham, Ontario.

Printed in the United States of America

10 9 8 7 6 5 4 3 2

Library of Congress Cataloging-in-Publication Data

Julian, of Norwich, b. 1343.
  A lesson of love.

  Translation of: Revelations of divine love.
  1. Devotional literature. I. John-Julian,
Father, O.J.N. II. Title.
BV4831.J8   1988   242   88-237
ISBN 0-8027-1029-8

This work has been dedicated
to gentle Robert, who brought me the ubiquity of the love;
to dear Julia, who gave me the priesthood of the woman;
to kindly Sheila, who sang me the beauty of the word;
and
to beloved Silas, who passed me by on the Way.

INTRODUCTION

It is the prophetic Herbert O'Driscoll who said, "Julian is not only a great lady of the past; she is also a great woman in our future. What Thomas Merton was to spirituality in the 1960s and 1970s, Julian of Norwich will be to the 1980s and 1990s."[1] And Merton himself wrote: ". . . Julian is without doubt one of the most wonderful of all Christian voices. She gets greater and greater in my eyes as I grow older and whereas in the old days I used to be crazy about St. John of the Cross, I would not exchange him now for Julian if you gave me the world and the Indies and all the Spanish mystics rolled up in one bundle. I think that Julian of Norwich is with Newman the greatest English theologian."[2]

What is it about this retiring, obscure, fourteenth-century English anchoress which stirs the hearts and minds of some of the greatest spiritual leaders of our time? What is it that has motivated some fourteen books to be published about Julian in the last few years (after almost 600 years of silence)? What spark has she struck in the imaginations and in the souls of moderns which has brought her finally into the very forefront of contemporary spirituality?

There can be no doubt but that the answer is contained in the pages of this book—in her own account of the miraculous revelations granted her during her seemingly mortal illness, and her long-awaited and carefully considered understandings of the meaning and implication of those visions. And the answer cannot finally be given perfectly by anyone except Julian herself.

However, since our primary goal in this new translation of her work is to increase her accessibility to contemporary readers, it might be helpful for us to suggest some of the themes and patterns of thought and theology which spring from her insights and her understandings of this "Lesson of Love" she received from her Lord. We do not pretend to speak *for* Julian—she speaks too well for herself—but we want here merely to point out some of Julian's primary lines of thought so that readers may be sensitive to the uniqueness of her understandings and to their amazing relevance to our lives today.

Optimism

First, and most obviously, Julian is a theological optimist. Standing over against the pessimism and sin-absorption of the popular theology of much of the Middle Ages—and in spite of living in the midst of devastating cultural revolution and the collapse of centuries-old institutions and patterns of life on which whole cultures had been based—Julian stands forward astoundingly as a primary voice of hope.

When we think of the events during her life in England, the parallels with our own time present themselves with awesome clarity. She saw the assassination of a king and an archbishop; she saw the nationwide rioting of the poor in the Peasants' Rebellion (and the harsh suppression of that movement—especially by her own military bishop Herbert le Despenser of Norwich); in her lifetime, she lived through three sieges of the Black Death, which struck Norwich with exceptional devastation and killed over half of the population there; she saw the beginning of the Hundred Years' War between England and France; she saw the firm rock of the papacy come crashing down—first in the Babylonian Captivity at Avignon, and later in the Great Schism, when for a time there were three men, each claiming to be the true Pope; she watched the continuing degeneration of the monasteries from being centers of the highest sacrifice and devotion to becoming England's greatest (and most self-aggrandizing) landlords; she saw the results of the moral collapse of the Friars (in whom so many had placed such high hopes); and she lived during the rise of England's first heretics in the persons of Oxford's John Wycliff and his later Lollard followers (some of whom were executed in the Lollard's Pit in Mousehold Heath at the edge of Norwich).

This was the mad, crumbling world in which this exceptional woman lived, and it was in this world that, astoundingly, she was able to accept and articulate those most famous words "All shall be well, and all shall be well, and all manner of thing shall be well."

But there is in Julian's optimism nothing of the self-blinding Pollyanna—nothing of the "make-believer" who simply converts pain, suffering, and sin into fictions, and pretends they are not real. Julian's "all shall be well" does NOT suggest that "tomorrow things will be better," but that in that Great Day, God's will *shall* ultimately be worked in all His creation and that even now, "the sweet eye of pity and of love never departs from us, and the working of mercy ceases not."[3] Her optimism is one of solid faith and absolute conviction, and the refusal to believe that the muddle and violence of earth is the final and exhaustive expression of reality.

We like to describe Julian as an "originist"—one who bears witness against our own inclinations to think that what a thing *does* is always what it *is*. If Julian were asked "What is a human being?" she would not base her answer merely on empirical observations of human foibles (although those would not escape her), but she would answer first by describing human *origins:* the gift of humanity given first by the Father to the Son before all time (the "first creation" of our human "essence" by God in heaven) then God's bonding of that human essence with our "soul" and our "fleshliness" in our birth, then our being "bought again" by Christ and reincorporated utterly into Him.

And her conclusion would be that humanity is of almost utmost value and worth—that humanity is the supreme creation of God, the divine gift of the divine Father to the divine Son, possessed of a "divine will that never consents to sin, nor ever will,"[4] virtually participating in the divinity of the Trinity itself. Julian would follow the now-unpopular Scholastic traditions of differentiating clearly between action, or function, and essence, or being. Regardless of what humans *do*, Julian knows what they *are*—and they are *very* good.

In a contemporary world in which we oscillate between seeing the human being as, on the one hand, the space-conquering semi-divine wonder-worker and, on the other hand, the holocaust-making, disgusting monster, Julian's vision reclaims reality for us. Sin *is* inevitable, and yet there is in us the divine will. We err, we fall, but we are only defined truly by the ceaseless and changeless loving of us by our Creator/Redeemer, not as gods, but as God-made men and women.

The existential horror of which humanity has proven itself capable is not the last word for Julian. There is more to be said in her conviction that we, vulnerable as we are to sin, are perfectible—that we carry the seed of that perfection from the moment of our creation, beneath even the most horrific sins.

Transcendence of History

Can you imagine a twentieth-century spiritual writer who made no comment on current social events? And yet there is not a single specific mention of any of her world's turmoil in Julian's writings! The reason is what we would describe as Julian's "transcendence of events." Any specific historical occurrence is of relative unimportance to one who does not worry and has no anxiety about those events!

Julian's transcendence is NOT a repudiation of pain, suffering, and turmoil (for we see even in the examples she uses that she knows those things well), but it is a "passing beyond" those earthly things, a refusal to be trapped by them, in the unswerving quiet confidence that "truly He does and causes every thing that is done."[5] There is, for Julian, no need to maunder and moan about circumstances and historical events, because whatever those circumstances or whatever those events, they are there at the will of God and in the hand of God, and "our heavenly Mother Jesus cannot allow us that are His children to perish."[6]

Indeed, she shows her assurance that her Lord will "give us more light and solace in heavenly joy by drawing our hearts from the sorrow and darkness which we are in."[7] In her long parable of the lord and the servant, Julian recognizes that one of the pains suffered by the fallen servant is that he is blinded by his own trouble and pain to such a degree that he cannot see the loving face of his lord as it looks upon him.[8] And Julian would struggle to avoid the same myopia of allowing herself to become blinded by the events of her day. In the context of the permanent and unflagging love of God, and absolute confidence in His will, Julian need not lose sight of the eternal forest for the circumstantial trees.

There is in her work no indication of a diversion of her devotion and/or a compromise of her total commitment to what was, in fact, an increasingly corrupt institutional Church. There is in Julian not a shred of anti-clericalism or of anti-institutionalism. Although some critics have striven to "modernize" Julian by dressing her in the garb of crypto-Protestantism or anti-clericalism, they are dead wrong. Time and time again, she deeply honors and unquestionably respects the systematized truths, teachings, and practices of Holy Church—while recognizing that those truths may be misused or misapplied (e.g., she mentions prayers which can be "said coarsely with the mouth, without the devout intention and wise effort which we owe to God in our prayers"[9]).

Julian was able to do what any Christian person today longs to do: to transcend the madness of the world, to see through its insanity and pass beyond it to the eternal verities, to live *sub specie æterni-tatis* in the midst of worldly rot, death, and collapse. Indeed, it is our conviction that this offering of a mystical transcendence (which allows one to make sense of external madness) is a major element which draws us moderns to this woman. When circumstances of the world are no longer sane, and when they have moved beyond one's personal power to change, one either leaps into the madness oneself, or one finds the route through and past it to the planes of reality, sanity, and order. And that Julian offers us.

No Wrath in God

In the face of TV evangelism, Julian's uncompromising proposition that "our Lord was never angry, nor ever shall be"[10] speaks wonder-fully to the guilt-ridden, parent-transferring Christian of today. Julian is blatant (almost a little "short" with potential opponents): ". . . He cannot be angry. It would be impossible."[11] For Julian, God is never a judgmental Daddy—writ large! And with a psychological acumen far in advance of her time, she declares that the reason we tend to see wrath in God is because the wrath is in us,[12] and that in our own blindness, we project and attribute our wrath to God.

Here Julian teaches a pure classical Christian theology—nearly forgotten today in the rush of mindless fundamentalism and the denial of mystical reality—God is impassible, totally unassailable by any passion (such as anger), and ever unchangeable (not subject, for instance, to a beginning and or ending of "wrath"). The familiar "wrathful God" is an Old Testament God—one described in that Kindergarten of God's revelation of Himself—and not the God of perfect Love manifested at Bethlehem and on Calvary. In a time when "God's judgment" is being hurled at us from every electronic pulpit, Julian's assurance that wrath is contrary to the entire char-acter of God is a fine balance and reminder of Him who said, "I did not come to judge the world but to save the world."[13] Julian's revelations are, in fact, all concerned with that divine love.

Christ Our Mother

Julian's unapologetic treatment of Christ as Mother is, without doubt, the finest and most sophisticated treatment of that subject in ALL of Christian literature.[14] It is only our contemporary ignorance of the classical Christian mystics and theologians, however, that leads us to think of this as a "new idea" for Julian—it is a venerable tradition supported by Adam of Perseigne, Aelred, Albert the Great, Anselm, Aquinas, Augustine, Bernard of Cluny, Bonaventure, Bridget of Sweden, Catherine of Siena, Clement of Alexandria, Dante, William Flete, Gilbert of Hoyland, Guerric of Igny, Guigo II the Carthusian, Helinand of Froidmont, Isaas of Stella, Margery Kempe, Peter Lombard, Ludolph of Saxony, Marguerite of Oingt, Mechtild of Magdeburg, Richard Rolle, William of St. Thierry, the *Ancren Riwle,* the *Stimulus Amoris,* and Holy Scripture itself.[15] It is not, therefore, surprising that Julian should present this idea as unexceptional—not as some devastatingly radical concept.

And we do a great injustice to Mother Julian if we assign to her even the faintest "feminist" motivations or intentions in the declaration of Christ's Motherhood. Julian's tradition, rather, comes from her identification of the Second Person of the Trinity with the traditional character of Wisdom—interpreted in all the Judeo-Christian tradition as the Divine Feminine[16] and from her understanding of the identity between "Mother Church" and the Mystical Body of Christ. For Julian, Christ *is* the Church, and the Church is the Mother. Christ *is* Wisdom, and Wisdom is the feminine.

And Julian does most modernists one better by a simple grammatical operation: she never uses anything but *masculine* pronouns in referring to Christ, so we have such wonderfully mystical and grammatically paradoxical statements of androgyny as "Our Mother Jesus, He . . ." This approach maintains the mystical and theological balance far better than declaring for a "female Jesus." However, Julian does not hesitate to be graphic about her mystical symbolism, and at one point declares: "He carries us within Himself in love, and labors full term. . . ."[17]

And Julian goes even a step further in that she never characterizes Christ as "like our mother," but the direct *opposite*—she describes motherhood (as she describes humanity itself) as pre-existing in Christ. Our mothers and what we call "mother love" are only emanations and imitations of Christ's own eternal and timeless Motherhood. Christ is the proto-Mother, and earthly motherhood (like all other earthly virtue) is merely an imitation and reflection of Him. Indeed, Julian goes so far as to say that it is even Christ who actually does our birthing when our natural mothers give us birth![18] Motherhood, Julian would say, is not a characteristic of womankind that Christ shares, but a characteristic of Christ which women share! And she declares that our natural responsibility to fatherhood and motherhood has its origin in the Fatherhood and Motherhood of God, and that responsibility is met by loving the Father/Mother God.[19]

In our own cultural struggle toward equality between sexes, Julian provides us with the best (and most metaphysical) basis of all for such equality—why should the feminine be as honored and as respected as the masculine? Because they are both divine! They are both attributes of the God we worship. And it is clearly our repudiation of the feminine in God which has allowed the Church to raise its armies, to burn those who diverge from its codified and canonical "truth," and to develop a God who is primarily a lawyer and a judge!

And, while truly submitting herself to Holy Church, Julian does not hesitate to value, trust, and teach her *own* insights as valid truth, too. In the superseded "short version" of her revelations, Julian expresses the culturally-predictable denigration of her womanhood—but when she comes to compose her final word, she omits that denigration altogether, and *dares* her book—dares the first book in history ever by a woman in English, dares it in the face of cultural disapproval of a woman's doing theology, dares her Middle English in the face of the cultural expectation that any valid theological writing would be in Latin, and dares even to express and live with some paradoxes which she refuses to resolve simply in favor of "masculine, rational order," and although she accepts the literary convention of generic male pronouns, on many occasions she dares clearly stating the balance (i.e., "If a man *or woman* were to . . .").

Not only does the theological and ideological content of her writing honor the feminine, but the phenomenon of her very writing itself carries that message clearly and unequivocally.

Sin Has No Substance

In her own discomfort with an apparently oversimplified view of the place of sin, Julian faced the terrible paradox of God's goodness, the horrific evidence of the world's evil and the knowledge of damnation. Uniquely, she is led to a way of living *in that paradox.*

How in the face of God's apparent total goodness and God's apparent total power, could there continue to be sin and damnation? This was a contradiction which Julian longed to resolve—and which she finally brought to resolution in her own mystical and absolutely unique way, once again, in Merton's words, "This is, for her, the heart of theology: *not solving the contradiction, but remaining in the midst of it,* in peace, knowing that it *is* fully solved, but that the solution is secret [in God], and will never be guessed until it is revealed [emphasis added]."[20]

One catches a clear flavor of this in her simple statement: "God cannot forgive"[21]—because He already has! She is not trapped by appearances or circumstances, but bases her convictions on a solid faith.

In consciousness of the other world of Higher Reality, Julian can declare that "I believe [sin][22] has no manner of essence nor any portion of being"—that it is no-thing—that it is "no deed"[23]—that all of us carry within our souls a "divine will" which *imago dei* "never consented to sin nor ever shall" and "is so good that it can never will evil, but always good"[24]—that we are enclosed, enfolded, enwrapped, enclothed constantly in God—that at all times God is "nearer to us than our own soul"[25]—that He is with us in the highest of our spiritual flights and the lowest of our physical needs (surely no conceit could be more powerful or graphic or even shocking to a modern mind than Julian's declaration of God's presence with us even in the process of bodily elimination!). Sin is only known by the pain it produces, and we are protected in our Friend's hand.

To those of us who blanch at the too-evident sin of human beings and who can find no comfort or hope in a hateful, vengeful, and punishing God, Julian introduces the power of faith. "Look," she would say, "you have faith in the immeasurable goodness and power of God, but in the face of that you can't understand the existence and power of sin and its resulting pain—forget trying to 'understand' it. Trust that faith of yours, and leave the understanding of the paradox to God's own revelation in His own time. He knows all that you know, and He has it all under control."

God Will Work His Will

Finally, her understanding of the solution to the unassailable and ubiquitous evil of the world against which one seems impotent is the clear awareness and utter belief that all that is done on earth is done or allowed by God, that God shall not fail to work His will, and that "God's word shall be preserved in all things."[26]

It seems that Julian's awareness goes somewhat beyond the classical concept of the "permissive will of God" (which simply *allows* evil to happen) to an even more positive sense that whatever we perceive as evil in the world has already, by the time we perceive it, been converted by God in His foreseeing wisdom and power into an outright good! In that commitment of faith, one can say that at a mystical level the only evil in the world is our own choice to be separated from God.

In answer to our technological and rationalistic cry "How can that be?" comes her word of certain faith—that God shall do a Secret Deed which we cannot know until it is done (an *eschatological secret,* Merton calls it)—and all *shall* ultimately be well.

We are cautioned by Julian several times not to "busy ourselves" to try to find out what that Great Deed will be (a caution disregarded by any number of commentators on Julian who supposedly respect her but apparently do not take her seriously, and who foolishly and pointlessly try to make guesses that the Great Deed may be "universal salvation" or "a new creation" or what-have-you).[27] I suspect that Julian's answer to those queries would simply be that what the Great Deed will be is God's business and not ours, and that is more than enough for a person of faith to know. For Julian, the knowledge that what God wills *will* finally come about is comfort and enough.

Mysticism Without Histrionics

In our dilemma, Julian offers to us neither a sociological solution nor a psychological solution nor a technological solution nor a political solution. She doesn't even offer us a simply religious or theological solution, but a *mystical* solution.

She guides us back to our forgotten spiritual roots, to the transcendence which is ours by virtue of our creation by the Father and our re-creation in the Son, back to the vision of reality we have almost lost in the thickets of technology and rationalism. She calls us to look beyond the misery and the sin to the divine frame in which these evil displays are seen—the frame of God's creation, God's love, and God's constant protection. He is *always* "our Maker, our Keeper, our Lover." She speaks for us in saying that there IS no solution to the hellish experience of our world in any terms in which we have learned to seek solutions—but only in the rediscovery of the unqualified and transcendent love of God. The wrath is not in God, but in us; the blindness is not divine, but human; the judgment is not heavenly, but earthly.

And for this woman there are no rolled-back eyeballs, no writhings on flagstone floors, no dubious analogues of divine sexual intercourse, no induced trances, no levitations or bi-locations, no magicianship, no extravagant and unattainable hyperboles, and no denials of *any* aspect of humanity or human experience. She neither displays nor asks us to participate in any Mediterranean extremities or Desert ascetics. Her understanding is utterly sharp, orderly, and clear, and her spirituality works by transcending, not by denying, the daily reality.

prayer, but the eighteenth/nineteenth-century idea (springing from the followers of the Wesleys) that unless prayer is constantly "heartfelt" it is invalid would have made her smile.

God is much more pleased, according to Julian, when our prayer is *unrewarding* to us but is centered on Him, rather than on our self-oriented personal "experience" or lack of same. "Praying," she declares, "is a true, gracious, lasting intention of the soul one-ed and made fast to the will of our Lord by the sweet, secret working of the Holy Spirit"[30]—a simple act of faithful and trust-filled willing, not the emotional experience of "gushing over Jesus."

She attributes "failure" in prayer to "our feeling, our foolishness,"[31] not to an inadequate method or insufficient emotions. We are delivered, by Julian, from the guilt of not *feeling* prayerful. In a direct analogy, one may often not *feel* like going home to one's spouse, but one goes home nevertheless out of faithfulness, and thereby demonstrates a love that transcends the myth of romance and the sentimentality of emotions. Good Thomist that she is, Julian knows that loving and praying are both done with the will, not the present in our very nature, in our very soul, but often invisible because of our own inadequate sight.

Julian would have a word for the Death-of-God theorists, and it would be that it is only the great shadow of our own mortality, with its present shallowness, its inadequacy, its ridiculous pride, which "requires" that God prove Himself to us on our non-spiritual terms. We are concerned by what we think about God; Julian *knows* what God thinks about us, and that far outshines our self-centered presumption.

Prayer

In opposition to our present devotion to sensation, Julian makes the case for true prayer—which, in her words, is usually and predictably "barren and dry" (and, indeed, may leave us as "barren and dry" when we have finished it as when we began):[28] Julian surely honors the presence of "devout intention and wise effort"[29] in our

Blindness

"Blindness" is Julian's favorite characterization of our failings—and it is an important one for a modern Christian. We who are constantly assailed by the phenomenological, the existential, and the empirical have a hard time thinking of God as One whom we do not generally experience. In our overweening cult of self, we seem to demand God's manifestation to us on our terms, and we have forgotten that for at least 1500 years of Christian history, the experience of the "Absence of God" (or the lack of experience of the Presence) would be attributed not to a failure on God's part, but to a failure on the part of humankind. And that "failure" from Julian's point of view is our *blindness!*

God surrounds us, enfolds us, encloses us—and most of the time we do not know it because we are not looking or seeing the Reality on Which we are grounded and in Which we are immersed. There is no wrathful withdrawing of God, there is only sinful myopia on our parts. God is not dead and not "gone" for Julian, He is utterly emotions. We are reminded, again, of Thomas Merton's words: "Pure love and prayer are learned in the hour when prayer has become impossible and your heart has turned to stone."

One needs now to get out of the way and to leave the reader with this astounding woman herself—whose work has been called by one bishop "the quintessence of English spirituality." She has lain quiet and still for 600 years, contemplatively awaiting the moment when the world's needs would call her again from the Avalon of her anchorhold cell—that tiny cell which contains the cosmos.

John-Julian, O.J.N.
Norwich, Connecticut
1987

---

1. Quoted in *14th Century English Mystics Newsletter*. Vol. IX, No. 4, Dec., 1983.

2. *Seeds of Destruction;* New York; Farrar, Strauss; 1964; pgs. 274–5.
3. Chapter 48.
4. Chapter 53.
5. Chapters 1 and 11.
6. Chapter 61.
7. Chapter 86.
8. Chapter 51.
9. Chapter 69.
10. Chapter 43.
11. Chapter 49.
12. Chapter 48: "I saw no wrath except on man's part . . . we . . . have in us a wrath and a continuing opposition to peace and love."
13. John 12:47.
14. Bynum, Caroline Walker; *Jesus as Mother;* Berkeley; Univ. of California; 1984; page 140.
15. From listings in Bynum and in Colledge and Walsh; *Showings;* New York; Paulist; 1978. Also, cf. Isaiah 66:13, Matthew 23:37, etc.
16. Cf. the excellent treatment of the character of Wisdom in Samuel Terrien's *The Elusive Presence;* San Francisco; Harper & Row; 1978.
17. Chapter 60.
18. Chapter 60: "though it is true that our bodily birth is but little, lowly, and simple compared to our spiritual birth, yet it is He wno does it within the created mothers by whom it is done."
19. Chapter 60: ". . . all our debt that we owe by God's bidding to fatherhood and motherhood, because of God's Fatherhood and Motherhood is fulfilled in the loving of God . . ."
20. *Conjectures of a Guilty Bystander;* Garden City; Doubleday; 1966; page 192.
21. Chapter 49.
22. Chapter 27.
23. Chapter 11.
24. Chapter 37.
25. Chapter 55.
26. Chapter 32.
27. Chapter 33: ". . . the more we busy ourselves to know His secrets in this or any other thing, the farther shall we be from the knowledge of them."
28. Chapter 41.
29. Chapter 69.
30. Chapter 41.
31. Chapter 41.

The incipit of the short text of the *Revelations*. The note immediately above identifies the author as "Julyan, that is recluse at Norwich and is yet alive, A.D. 1413." (British Library, London, Additional MS 37790, f. 97)

16 The XVI shews ${y}$ ${yt}$ the blissfull Trinity
our maker, in X^t Jesus our Savior endles-
ly dwelleth in our Souls worshipfully,
ruling and giving us all things mightily,
& wisely saving and keeping us for love, so
that we shall not be overcome of our
Enimy.

The 2 Chapter:
Of ${y}$ time of these Revelations.
& how she asked three Petitions.

These Revelations were shewed to a simple
Creature, that could no letter in ${y}$ year of
of Lord 1373, the 8th day of May, which
Creature desired before, three gifts of
God. the first was Mende of his passion;
${y}$ 2cond was bodily sikness in youth att 30
years of age; ${y}$ 3d. was to have of God's
gift 3 wounds.

1 As to ${y}$ first methought I had some feeling
in

Revelations

shown to one who could not read a letter.
Anno Domini, 1373.

1

A detailed list of the chapters.

This is a revelation of love that Jesus Christ, our endless joy, made in sixteen showings or revelations, in detail, of which

The first is concerning His precious crowning with thorns;
and therewith was included and described in detail
the Trinity with
the Incarnation and
the unity between God and man's soul,
with many beautiful showings of endless wisdom and
teachings of love in which all the showings that follow are
based and united.

The second showing is the discoloring of His fair face in symbolizing His dearworthy passion.

The third showing is that our Lord God—
all Power,
all Wisdom,
all Love
—just as truly as He has made every thing that is, also truly He does and causes every thing that is done.

The fourth showing is the scourging of His frail body with abundant shedding of His blood.

The fifth showing is that the Fiend is overcome by the precious Passion of Christ.

The sixth showing is the honor-filled favor of our Lord God with which He rewards all His blessed servants in heaven.

The seventh showing is a frequent experience of well and woe—
the experience of "well" is grace-filled touching and enlightening, with true certainty of endless joy;
the experience of "woe" is temptation by sadness and annoyance of our fleshly life—

with spiritual understanding that even so we are protected safely in love—in woe as in well—by the goodness of God.

The eighth showing is the last pains of Christ and His cruel dying.

The ninth showing is about the delight which is in the blessed Trinity because of the cruel Passion of Christ and His regretful dying; in this joy and delight He wills we be comforted and made happy with Him until when we come to the fullness in heaven.

The tenth showing is that our Lord Jesus shows his blessed heart equally cloven in two in love.

The eleventh showing is a noble, spiritual showing of His dearworthy Mother.

The twelfth showing is that our Lord is all supreme Being.

The thirteenth showing is that our Lord God wills that we have great regard for
all the deeds that He has done in the great splendor of creating all things, and
of the excellency of creating man (who is above all His other works), and
of the precious amends that He has made for man's sin, turning all our blame into endless honor,

2

and here also our Lord says:

"Behold and see;

for by the same Power, Wisdom, and Goodness that I have
done all this,

by that same Power, Wisdom, and Goodness I shall make
well all that is not well, and

thou thyself shalt see it."

And in this showing He wills that we keep us in the Faith and
truth of Holy Church, not wishing to be aware of His secrets
now, except as is proper for us in this life.

The fourteenth showing is that our Lord is the foundation of our
prayer. Herein were seen two elements which He wills both
be equally great:

the one is righteous prayer,

the other is sure trust;

and in these ways our prayer delights Him and He of His
goodness fulfills it.

The fifteenth showing is that

we shall without delay be taken from all our pain and from all
our woe and, of His goodness,

we shall come up above where we shall

have our Lord Jesus for our recompense,

and be filled with joy and bliss in heaven.

The sixteenth showing is that the blessed Trinity our Creator, in
Christ Jesus our Savior,

endlessly dwells in our soul,

honorably governing and controlling all things,

powerfully and wisely saving and protecting us for the
sake of love;

and that we shall not be overcome by our Enemy.

3

2

These revelations were shown to a simple creature that had learned
    no letter, in the year of our Lord, 1373, the 8th day of May.
This creature had previously desired three gifts from God:
   the first was memory of His passion;
   the second was bodily sickness in youth at thirty years of age;
   the third was to have from God's gift three wounds.

As for the first,
        I thought I had *some* sense of the passion of Christ, but still
        I desired more by the grace of God.

I thought that I wished to have been at that time with Mary
    Magdalen and with the others who were Christ's lovers,
and therefore I desired a bodily sight wherein I could have more
    knowledge
   of the bodily pains of our Savior, and
   of the compassion of Our Lady and
   of all His true lovers who at that time saw His pains,
   for I wished to be one of them and to suffer with them.

        I never desired any other sight or showing
        of God until the soul was departed from
        the body
      (for I believed to be saved by the mercy of God).

The purpose for this petition was so that after the showing I
would have a more true consciousness of the Passion of Christ.

The second gift came to my mind with contrition, freely without
    any effort:
       a willing desire to have from God's gift a bodily sickness.

I wished that the sickness would be so severe as to seem mortal
so that I could, in that sickness,
receive all my rites of Holy Church,
myself expecting that I should die,
and that all creatures who saw me could suppose the same
(for I wished to have no kind of comfort from earthly life).

In this sickness, I desired to have all the kinds of
pains, bodily and spiritual, that I would have if I
were to die, with all the fears and temptations
of the fiends—except the outpassing of the soul.

And this I intended so that
I would be purged by the mercy of God and
afterwards live more to the honor of God because of that
sickness,
for I hoped that it could be to my benefit when I would
have died
(for I desired to be soon with my God and Maker).

These two desires for the Passion and the sickness I desired of Him
with a condition
(for it seemed to me this was not the common custom of prayer)
saying thus:
"Lord, Thou knowest what I wish—if it be Thy will that I
have it;
and if it be not Thy will, good Lord, be not displeased,
for I want nothing except what Thou wilt."

For the third gift, by the grace of God and teaching of Holy Church,
I conceived a mighty desire to receive three wounds while I was
alive: that is to say,
the wound of true contrition,
the wound of natural compassion, and
the wound of wish-filled yearning for God.

5

And, just as I asked the other two with a condition,
so all this last petition I asked mightily without any condition.

The first two desires passed from my memory, but the third
dwelled with me constantly.

3

When I was thirty years old and a half, God sent me a bodily sickness
in which I lay three days and three nights;
and on the fourth night, I received all my rites of Holy Church
and expected not to have lived till day.

After this I lay two days and two nights.
And on the third night I expected often to have passed away
(and so expected they that were with me).

And being still in youth, I thought it a great sadness to die—
not for anything that was on earth that pleased me to live for,
nor for any pain that I was afraid of
(for I trusted in God of His mercy)
but because I would have liked to have lived so that I could have
loved God better and for a longer time,
so that I could have more knowledge and
love from God in the bliss of heaven.

For it seemed to me that all the time I had lived here—
so little and so short in comparison to that endless bliss—
I thought of as nothing.

Wherefore I thought:
"Good Lord, let my living no longer be to Thine honor!"

And I understood by my reason and by the experience of my pains
that I would die.

And I assented fully with all the will of my heart, to be at God's will.

Thus I endured till day,
  and by then my body was dead from the midst downwards as regards my feeling.
  Then was I aided to be set upright, supported with help, in order to have more freedom for my heart to be at God's will, and thinking of God while my life should last.

My curate was sent for to be at my ending, and by the time he came I had cast my eyes upwards and could not speak.
He placed the cross before my face and said:
  'I have brought thee the image of thy Maker and Savior.
  Look thereupon and comfort thyself with it."

It seemed to me that I was all right,
  for my eyes were set upwards to heaven
    (where I trusted to come by the mercy of God)
  but nevertheless I consented to fix my eyes on the face of the crucifix if I could,
  and so I did
    (for it seemed to me that I might longer endure to look straight forward than straight up).

After this my sight began to fail
  and it grew all dark about me in the chamber
    as if it had been night,
  except on the image of the cross on which I beheld an ordinary light, and I know not how.

Everything except the cross became ugly to me as if it had been much possessed by the fiends.

And after this the upper part of my body began to die so noticeably
    that scarcely had I any feeling—
my worst pain was shortness of breath and waning of life.

And then I expected truly to have passed away.

But, in the midst of this,
    suddenly all my pain was taken from me
    and I was as whole (especially in the upper part of my body) as
        ever I had been before.

I marveled at this sudden change
    (for it seemed to me that it was a secret act of God
        and not of nature)
but even with the feeling of this comfort, I trusted never the more
    to live;

    and the feeling of this comfort was no full ease to me,
        for it seemed to me I would rather have been delivered from
            this world,
        for my heart was wishfully set on that.

Then came suddenly to my memory
    that I should desire the second wound of our Lord's gracious gift:
        that my body could be filled with the memory and feeling of
        His blessed Passion, as I had prayed before
            (for I had wished that His pains were my pains with
            compassion, and, afterward, yearning for God).

Thus I thought I could with His grace
    have the wounds that I had desired before.

However, in this I never desired any bodily sight
    nor any kind of showing from God

(except compassion, such as a natural soul could have with our
Lord Jesus, who for the sake of love willed to be a mortal man).

And therefore I desired to suffer with Him, while living in my mortal
body, as God would give me grace.

4

In this showing suddenly I saw the red blood trickling down from
under the garland,
hot and freshly and most plenteously,
just as it was at the time of His Passion
when the garland of thorns was pressed onto His blessed head.

Just so, I conceived truly and powerfully that it was He Himself
(both God and man, the Same who suffered thus for me)
who showed it to me without any go-between.

And in the same showing suddenly the Trinity
almost filled my heart with joy.
(And I understood it shall be like that in heaven without end for
all that shall come there.)

For the Trinity is God, God is the Trinity;
the Trinity is our Maker,
the Trinity is our Keeper,
the Trinity is our everlasting Lover,
the Trinity is our endless Joy and Bliss,
by our Lord Jesus Christ.

(And this was shown in the first revelation and in all of them, for
wherever Jesus appears, the blessed Trinity is understood,
as I see it.)

And I said: *"Benedicite domine!"*
  (This I said, for reverence in my meaning,
  with a powerful voice,
  and full greatly astonished because of the wonder and amazement
      that I had that He who is so respected and awesome wished
      to be so familiar with a sinful creature living
      in this miserable flesh.)

Thus I understood that at that time our Lord Jesus out of His
    gracious love
  wished to show me comfort before the time of my temptation
      (for it seemed to me that it could well be that I would—
      by the permission of God and with His protection—
      be tempted by fiends before I died).

With this sight of His blessed Passion
  along with the Godhead that I saw in my understanding,
  I knew well that it was strength enough for me
      (yea, and for all creatures living that would be saved)
  against all the fiends of hell and spiritual temptation.

In this showing He brought Our Blessed Lady Saint Mary
    to my mind.
  I saw her spiritually in bodily likeness,
    a simple maid and humble,
    young of age and little grown beyond childhood,
    in the stature that she was when she conceived with child.

Also God showed in part the wisdom and the truth of her soul
  wherein I understood the reverent contemplation with which she
      beheld her God and Maker,
  marveling with great reverence that He wished to be born of her
      who was a simple creature of His own creation.

10

And this wisdom and truth
    (knowing the greatness of her Creator
    and the littleness of herself who is created)
    caused her to say full humbly to Gabriel:
    "Behold me here, God's handmaiden."

In this sight I understood truly
    that she is higher in worthiness and grace than all that God made
      beneath her,
    for nothing that is created is greater than she, except the blessed
      Manhood of Christ, as I see it.

5

At this same time that I saw this sight of the head bleeding, our good
    Lord showed to me a spiritual vision of His simple loving.

I saw that He is to us everything that is good and comfortable for us.
    He is our clothing which for love enwraps us,
      holds us,
    and all encloses us because of His tender love,
      so that He can never leave us.

And so in this showing I saw that He is to us everything that is good,
    as I understood it.

Also in this revelation He showed a little thing,
    the size of an hazel nut
    in the palm of my hand,
    and it was as round as a ball.

I looked at it with the eye of my understanding and thought:
    "What can this be?"

11

And it was generally answered thus: "It is all that is made."

I marveled how it could continue,
    because it seemed to me it could suddenly have sunk into nothing-
        ness because of its littleness.
And I was answered in my understanding:
    "It continueth and always shall, because God loveth it;
    and in this way *everything* hath its being by the love of God."

In this little thing I saw three characteristics:
    the first is that God made it,
    the second is that God loves it,
    the third, that God keeps it.

But what did I observe in that?
    Truly the Maker, the Lover, and the Keeper for,
        until I am in essence one-ed to Him,
        I can never have full rest nor true joy
    (that is to say,
        until I am made so fast to Him
        that there is absolutely nothing that is created
        separating my God and myself).

It is necessary for us to have awareness
    of the littleness of created things
        and to set at naught everything that is created,
        in order to love and have God who is uncreated.

For this is the reason why we are not fully at ease in heart and soul:
    because here we seek rest in these things that are so little,
        in which there is no rest,
    and we recognize not our God who is all powerful, all wise, all
        good, for He is the true rest.

God wishes to be known,
   and He delights that we remain in Him,
   because all that is less than He is not enough for us.

And this is the reason why no soul is at rest
   until it is emptied of everything that is created.
When the soul is willingly emptied for love
   in order to have Him who is all,
   then is it able to receive spiritual rest.

Also our Lord God showed
   that it is full great pleasure to Him
   that a pitiable soul come to Him nakedly and plainly and simply.
      For this is the natural yearning of the soul,
      thanks to the touching of the Holy Spirit,
      according to the understanding that I have in this showing—
         "God, of Thy goodness, give me Thyself;
            for Thou are enough to me,
            and I can ask nothing that is less
            that can be full honor to Thee.
         And if I ask anything that is less,
            ever shall I be in want,
            for only in Thee have I all."

These words are full lovely to the soul
   and most nearly touch upon the will of God and His goodness,
      for His goodness fills all His creatures and all His blessed works,
      and surpasses them without end,
      for He is the endlessness.

And He has made us only for Himself
   and restored us by His blessed passion
   and ever keeps us in His blessed love.

And all this is from His goodness.

13

6

This showing was made to teach our soul wisely to cleave to the goodness of God.

At that time the custom of our praying was brought to mind:
how, for lack of understanding and recognition of love,
we are used to creating many intermediaries.

Then saw I truly that it is more honor to God and more true delight
that we faithfully pray to Himself out of His goodness,
and cleave to that goodness by His grace with true understanding
and steadfast belief,
than if we created all the intermediaries that heart can think of.

For if we create all these intermediaries,
it is too little,
and not complete honor to God,
whereas all the whole of it is in His goodness,
and there absolutely nothing fails.

For this, as I shall say, came to my mind at the same time:
we pray to God
by His Holy Flesh
and by His Precious Blood,
His Holy Passion,
His dearworthy Death and Wounds,
by all His blessed Human Nature,
but the endless life that we have from all this is from His goodness.

And we pray to Him by His sweet Mother's love who bore Him,
but all the help we have from her is of His goodness.

And we pray by His Holy Cross that He died on,
    but all the strength and the help that we have from the cross is
        from His goodness.

And in the same way, all the help that we have from special saints
    and all the blessed company of heaven—
the dearworthy love and endless friendship that we have from
    them—it is from His goodness.

For God of His goodness has ordained intermediaries to help us,
    all fair and many,
    of which the chief and principal intermediary is the blessed Human
        Nature that He took from the Maid,
    with all the intermediaries that go before and come after which
        are part of our redemption and our endless salvation.

Wherefore it pleases Him
    that we seek Him and worship Him by intermediaries,
    understanding and recognizing that He is the goodness of all.

For the goodness of God is the highest prayer and it comes down to
    the lowliest part of our need.

    It vitalizes our soul
    and brings it to life
    and makes it grow in grace and virtue.

    It is nearest us in nature
    and readiest in grace
        (for it is the same grace that the soul seeks and ever shall,
        till we know our God truly who has us all in Himself enclosed).

A man goes upright
    and the food of his body is sealed as in a purse full fair;

and when it is time of his necessity, it is opened
and sealed again full honestly.
And that it is He who does this is shown there where He says that
He comes down to us to the lowest part of our need.

For He does not despise what He has created,
and He does not disdain to serve us even at the simplest duty that
is proper to our body in nature, because of the love of our soul
which He has made in His own likeness.

For as the body is clad in the clothes,
and the flesh in the skin,
and the bones in the flesh,
and the heart in the breast,
so are we, soul and body, clad in the goodness of God and
enclosed—yea, and even *more* intimately,
because all these others may waste and wear away,
but the goodness of God is ever whole,
and nearer to us without any comparison.

For truly our Lover desires that our soul cleave to Him with all its
might and that we evermore cleave to His goodness,
for of all things that heart can think,
this pleases God most and soonest succeeds.

For our soul is so especially beloved by Him that is Highest that it
surpasses the knowledge of all creatures
(that is to say, there is no creature that is made that can know
how much and how sweetly and how tenderly our Creator loves
us).

Therefore we can, with His grace and His help, remain in spiritual
contemplation, with everlasting wonder at this high, surpassing,
inestimable love which Almighty God has for us of His goodness.

16

And therefore we can ask of our Lover with reverence
    all that we wish,
  for our natural wish is to have God
  and the good wish of God is to have us.

And we can never leave off wishing nor longing until we have Him in
    fullness of joy,
    and then can we wish for nothing more,
  for He wills that we be occupied
  in knowing and loving
  until the time that we shall be fulfilled in heaven.

      And for this purpose was this lesson of love shown (along
      with all that follows, as you shall see)—for the
      strength and the basis of all was shown in the first
      vision.

For of all things,
  the beholding and the loving of the Creator
    makes the soul seem less in its own sight,
    and most fills it with reverent fear and true humility,
    with an abundance of love for its fellow Christians.

7

And to teach us this, as I understand it, our lord God showed
Our Lady Saint Mary at the same time
    (which is to signify the exalted wisdom and truth she had
    in contemplating her Creator
      so great,
      so high,
      so mighty,
      and so good).

This greatness and this nobility of her vision of God filled her with
reverent fear
  and with this she saw herself
    so little and so lowly,
    so simple and so poor, in relation to her Lord God,
  that this reverent dread filled her with humility.

And thus, for this reason, she was filled full of grace
      and of all kinds of virtues
      and surpasses all creatures.

During all the time that He showed this which I have just described
in spiritual vision, I was watching the bodily sight of the abundant
bleeding of the Head continuing.
  The great drops of blood fell down from under the garland
    like pellets, seeming as if they had come out of the veins;
   and as they emerged they were brown-red
    (for the blood was very thick)
    and in the spreading out they were bright red;
  and when the blood came to the brows,
   there the drops vanished;
  and nevertheless the bleeding continued
   until many things were seen and understood.

  The beauty and the lifelikeness was comparable to nothing except
    itself.
  The abundance was like the drops of water that fall off the eaves
    of a house after a great shower of rain which fall so thick that
    no man can number them with earthly wit.
  And because of their roundness, the drops were like the scales of
    herring as they spread over the forehead.

    These three things came to my mind at the time:
      pellets, because of roundness, in the emerging of the blood;

the scales of herring, in the spreading over the forehead,
and because of the roundness;
the drops off the eaves of a house, because of the
immeasurable abundance.

This showing was alive and active,
and hideous and dreadful,
and sweet and lovely.

And of all the sights it was most comfort to me that our
God and Lord,
who is so worthy of respect
and so fearsome,
is also so plain and gracious;
and this filled me almost full with delight and security of soul.

For the interpretation of this He showed me this clear example: it is
the most honor that a solemn king or great lord can do for a
poor servant if he is willing to be friendly with him, and,
specifically, if he demonstrates it himself, from a full, true
intention, and with a glad countenance, both privately and
publicly. Then thinks this poor creature thus: "Ah! How could
this noble lord give more honor and joy to me than to show me,
who am so little, this marvelous friendliness? Truly, it is more
joy and pleasure to me than if he gave me great gifts and were
himself distant in manner."
This bodily example was shown so mightily that man's heart could be
carried away and almost forget itself for joy over this great
friendliness.

Thus it fares between our Lord Jesus and ourselves;
for truly it is the most joy that can be, as I see it,
that He who is highest and mightiest,
noblest and worthiest,
is also lowliest and meekest,
most friendly and most gracious.

19

And surely and truly this marvelous joy shall be shown us all when we see Him. And this wishes Our Lord:
  that we believe and trust,
     enjoy and delight,
     comfort and solace ourselves, as best we can,
     with His grace and with His help,
     until the time that we see that joy truly.

For the greatest fullness of joy that we shall have, as I see it, is the
     marvelous graciousness and friendliness
  of our Father who is our Creator,
  in our Lord Jesus Christ who is our Brother and our Savior.

But no man can be aware of this marvelous friendliness in this life,
  unless he receives it by special showing from Our Lord,
  or from a great abundance of grace inwardly given from the
     Holy Spirit.

But faith and belief with love are worthy to have the reward,
  and so it is received by grace—
  for in faith with hope and love, our life is grounded.

The showing (made to whom God wishes) plainly teaches the same, uncovered and explained with many secret points which are parts of our Faith and Belief which it is honorable to know. And when the showing, which is given at one time, is past and hidden, then the Faith keeps it by the grace of the Holy Spirit until our life's end.

And this is the showing—it is none other than the Faith, neither less nor more
  (as can be seen by our Lord's meaning in the earlier matter)
  until it comes to the final end.

8

As long as I saw this sight of the plenteous bleeding of the head, I could never cease these words: *"Benedicite domine!"*

In this showing of the bleeding I interpreted six things:
>   the first is the sign of the blessed Passion and the plenteous shedding of His Precious Blood;
>   the second is the Maiden who is His dearworthy Mother;
>   the third is the blessed Godhead that ever was, is, and ever shall be, all Power, all Wisdom, all Love;
>   the fourth is everything that He has created (for well I know that heaven and earth and all that is created is ample and large, fair and good,
>   but the reason why it appeared so little in my vision was because I saw it in the Presence of Him who is the Creator of all things, and to a soul that sees the Creator of everything, all that is created seems very little);
>   the fifth is that He created everything for love
>   and by the same love everything is protected
>   and shall be without end;
>   the sixth is that God is everything that is good, as I see it,
>   and the goodness that everything has, it is He.

All this our Lord showed me in the first vision
>   and gave me time and space to contemplate it,
>   and the bodily sight ceased,
>   and the spiritual sight remained in my understanding.

And I waited with reverent fear, rejoicing in what I saw.

And I desired, as much as I dared, to see more, if it were His will
>   (or else the same thing for a longer time).

In all this, I was much moved in love for my fellow Christians—that they could see and know the same that I saw, for I wish it to be a comfort to them—because all this sight was shown universally.

Then I said to those who were around me:
"It is Doomsday today for me."
(This I said because I expected to have died—for on the day that a man or woman dies, that person experiences the particular judgement as he shall be without end, as I understand it.)

I said this because I wished they would love God the better,
in order to remind them that this life is short,
as they might see in my example
(for in all this time I expected to have died, and that was a wonder to me and sad in part, because it seemed to me that this vision was shown for those who would live).

All that I say concerning myself, I say in the person of all my fellow Christians, for I am taught in the spiritual showing of our Lord God, that He intends it so.

Therefore I beg you all for God's sake,
and I advise you for your own benefit,
that you believe this vision of a sinner to whom it was shown,
and powerfully, wisely, and humbly look to God
who of His gracious love and endless goodness wishes to show the vision universally in reassurance for us all.

It is God's will that you receive it with great joy and delight since Jesus has shown it to you all.

9

I am not good because of this showing,
but only if I love God better;

and in so much as you love God better,
it is more to you than to me.

I do not say this to those who are wise, for they know it well,
but I say it to you who are simple,
for your benefit and comfort,
for we are all one in love.

Truly it was not shown to me that God loved me better than the least
soul that is in grace,
for I am certain that there are many who never had showing nor
vision (except from the common teaching of Holy Church)
who love God better than I.

If I look individually at myself, I am just nothing;
but in general terms, I am, I hope, in unity of love with all my
fellow Christians.

On this unity is based the lives of all mankind that shall be saved,
for God is all that is good, as I see it,
and God has created all that is created,
and God loves all that He has created,
and he who broadly loves all his fellow Christians because of God,
he loves all that is.

For in mankind that shall be saved is contained all
(that is to say, all that is created and the Creator of all)
because in man is God,
and in God is all,
and he who loves thus, loves all.

And I hope by the grace of God that he who sees it in this way shall
be truly taught and mightily comforted if he needs comfort.

I speak of those who shall be saved, because at this time God showed
me no other.

But in everything I believe as Holy Church believes, preaches, and teaches
  (for the Faith of Holy Church which I had beforehand believed
  and, as I hope, by the grace of God, willingly observe in use and custom, remained constantly in my sight)
wishing and intending never to accept anything that could be contrary to it.

And with this intent, I watched the showing with all my diligence,
  because in this whole blessed showing,
  I saw it as one with that Faith in God's intention.

All this was shown in three parts: that is to say,
  by bodily sight,
  and by word formed in my understanding,
  and by spiritual sight.
    (However, the spiritual sight I do not know how nor am I able
      to show it as openly nor as fully as I wish,
    but I trust in our Lord God Almighty that He shall of His
      goodness, and because of your love,
    cause you to receive it more spiritually and more sweetly than I
      know how or am able to tell it.)

10

And after this, I saw with bodily sight
  on the face of the crucifix which hung before me
    (on which I gazed constantly)
  a part of His Passion:
    contempt,
    and spitting
    and defiling
    and smiting
    and many distressing pains—more than I can count,
    and frequent changing of color.

And at the same time I saw how half the face, beginning at the ear, was overspread with dried blood until it was covered up to the middle of the face,

and after that, the other half was covered in the same way, and then it vanished in the first part just as it had come.

This I saw physically, sorrowfully and obscurely,
and I desired more physical light in order to have
seen more clearly.
But I was answered in my reason:
"If God wishes to show thee more, He shall be thy light.
Thou needest none but Him."

For I saw Him and still sought Him,

for we are now so blind and so unwise that we never seek God
until he of His goodness shows Himself to us;
and when we see anything of Him by grace, then are we moved by
the same grace to try with great desire
to see Him more perfectly.

And thus I saw Him and I sought Him,
and I possessed Him and I lacked Him.
And this is, and should be, our ordinary behavior in this life,
as I see it.

At one time my understanding was taken down into the sea-bed,
and there I saw hills and green dales,
seeming as if it were overgrown with moss,
with seaweed and gravel.

Then I understood this:
that even if a man or woman were there under the broad water,
if he could have a vision of God there
(since God is with a man constantly)

he would be safe in body and soul and receive no harm
and, even more, he would have more solace and more comfort
than all this world can tell.

Because He wills that we believe that we experience Him
constantly (although we imagine that it is but little)
and by this belief He causes us evermore to gain grace, because
He wishes to be seen and He wishes to be sought,
He wishes to be awaited and He wishes to be trusted.

This second showing was so lowly and so little and so simple that my
spirits were in great travail over the sight—mourning, fearful and
yearning—for I was sometimes even in doubt whether it was a
showing.

And then at different times our good Lord gave me more insight
whereby I understood truly that it was a showing.

It was a shape and image of our foul mortal flesh that our fair,
bright, blessed Lord bare for our sins.
It made me think of the holy Veronica's Veil of Rome which He
has imprinted with His own blessed face
(when He was in His cruel Passion, willingly going to His death)
and often changing color.

From the brownness and blackness, pitifulness and leanness of
this image, many marvel how it could be so, given that He
imprinted it with His blessed Face
which is the fairness of heaven,
the flower of earth,
and the fruit of the Maiden's womb.
Then how could this image be so discolored
and so far from fair?

I desire to say just as I have understood it by the grace of God.

We know in our Faith and believe by the teaching and preaching
of Holy Church that the entire blessed Trinity
created mankind in His image and to His likeness.

In the same sort of way we know that when man fell so deep and
so wretchedly by sin, there was no other help to restore man
except through Him who created man.

And He that created man for love, by the same love He wished to
restore man to the same bliss, and even more.

And just as we were created like the Trinity
in our first creation,
our Maker wished that we should be like Jesus Christ our Savior,
in heaven without end,
by the strength of our re-creation.

Then between these two He was willing
(for love and honor of man)
to make Himself as much like man in this mortal life
(in our foulness and our wretchedness)
as man could be without sins.

From this comes what the showing signifies.
As I said before, it was the image and likeness of our foul,
black, mortal flesh wherein our fair, bright, blessed Lord
hid His Godhead.
But most surely I dare to say (and we ought to believe) that
no man was as fair as He until the time that His fair
complexion was changed with toil and sorrow,
suffering and dying.

(Of this it is spoken in the eighth revelation where it tells more about
the same likeness—and there it says of the Veronica's Veil of

27

Rome, that it moves through different changes of color and
expression—
sometimes more reassuring and lifelike,
and sometimes more pitifully and deathly—
as can be seen in the eighth revelation.)

This vision was a teaching for my understanding
that the constant seeking of the soul pleases God very much;
for the soul can do no more than seek, suffer, and trust, and this is
brought about in the soul that has it by the Holy Spirit, but the
clarity of finding is by His special grace when it is His will.

The seeking with faith, hope, and love pleases our Lord,
and the finding pleases the soul and fills it full of joy.

And thus was I taught for my own understanding that seeking is as
good as beholding during the time that He wishes to permit the soul
to be in labor.

It is God's will that we seek Him until we behold Him,
for by that beholding He shall show us Himself
by His special grace
when He wishes.

How a soul shall behave itself in beholding Him,
He Himself shall teach;
and that is most honor to Him
and most benefit to the soul
and mostly received from humility and virtue
with the grace and leading of the Holy Spirit.

A soul that simply makes itself fast to God with true trust—either by
seeking or in beholding—that is the most honor that it can do to
Him, as I see it.

28

These are two workings which can be seen in this vision:
   the one is seeking,
   the other is beholding.
The seeking is universal so that every soul can have with His grace
(and ought to have) the moral discernment and teaching of the
   Holy Church.

It is God's will that we have three objects in our seeking:
   The first is that we seek willingly and diligently, without laziness,
      as much as possible through His grace, gladly and merrily
      without unreasonable sadness and useless sorrow.
   The second is that we await Him steadfastly because of His love,
      without grumbling or struggling against Him, until our life's
      end (for it shall last only a while).
   The third is that we trust in Him mightily in fully-certain faith, for
      it is His will that we know that He shall appear without
      warning and full of blessing to all His lovers—
   for His working is secret,
      but He wishes to be perceived,
   and His appearing shall be truly without warning,
      but He wishes to be trusted,
   because He is most simple and gracious.

Blessed may He be!

11

And after this, I saw God in a point
   (that is to say in my mind)
   by which vision I understood that He is in all things.

I gazed with deliberation,
   seeing and knowing in that vision that He does all that is done.

I marvelled at that sight with a mild fear, and thought: "What is sin?" (for I saw truly that God does everything no matter how little, and I saw truly that nothing is done by luck or by chance but everything by the foreseeing wisdom of God).

(If it is luck or chance in the sight of man, our blindness and our lack of foresight is the cause, for the things that are in the foreseeing wisdom of God from without beginning [which rightfully and honorably and constantly he leads to the best end as they come about] happen to us without warning, ourselves unaware; and thus, by our blindness and our lack of foresight, we say these are luck and chance; but to our Lord God, they are not so—
wherefore, it is necessary to concede that everything that is done, it is well done, for our Lord God does all
   [for at this time the action of creatures was not shown, but of our Lord God in the creature]).

He is in the midpoint of everything and He does everything, and I was certain He does no sin.

And here I saw truthfully that sin is no deed,
   for in all this revelation sin was not shown.

And I wished no longer to wonder at this, but I looked to our Lord for what He wished to show.

And thus insofar as could be shown for the present, the rightfulness of God's action was shown to the soul.

Rightfulness has two fair qualities:
   it is right,
   and it is full;
and so are all the actions of our Lord God;
and to them is lacking neither the action of mercy nor of grace,
for it is all right-full, in which nothing is wanting.

30

(And at a different time He made a showing in order for
me to see sin nakedly, as I shall say later, where He uses
the action of mercy and grace.)

This vision was shown to my understanding,
    for our Lord wished to have the soul turned truly
unto the beholding of Him,
and generally of all His works
    (for they are most good
    and all His judgments are comfortable and gracious,
    and they bring to great comfort the soul
        which has turned from paying attention to the blind judgment
            of man
        to the fair, gracious judgment of our Lord God).

A man looks upon some deeds as well done
    and some deeds as evil,
but our Lord does not look upon them so;

    for just as all that has being in nature is of God's creating,
    so everything that is done is in the character of God's doing.

It is easy to understand that the best deed is well done,
    but just as well as the best and most exalted deed is done,
    so well is the least deed done—
        and all in the character and in the order
      in which our Lord has it ordained from without beginning.

For there is no doer but He.

I saw full certainly that He never changes His purpose in anything,
    nor ever shall, without end.

There was nothing unknown to Him in His rightful ordering from
    without beginning,

and therefore everything was set in order before anything was
     created, just as it would stand without end,
and no manner of thing shall fall short of that mark.

He made everything in fullness of goodness,
     and therefore the Blessed Trinity is always completely pleased
          with all His works.

And all this He showed most blessedly, meaning this:
     "See, I am God.
     See, I am in everything.
     See, I do everything.
     See, I never lift my hands from my works, nor ever shall,
          without end.
     See, I lead everything to the end I ordained for it
          from without beginning
          by the same Power, Wisdom, and Love with which I made it.

How would anything be amiss?"

Thus powerfully, wisely, and lovingly was the soul tested
     in this vision.

Then I saw truthfully that it was appropriate that I needs must assent
with great reverence, rejoicing in God.

12

After this, as I watched, I saw the body plenteously bleeding
     (as could be expected from the scourging)
     in this way:
          the fair skin was split very deeply into the tender flesh by the
               harsh beating all over the dear body;
          so plenteously did the hot blood run out that one could see
               neither skin nor wound, but, as it were, all blood.

And when it came to the place where it should have fallen down,
there it vanished.

Nevertheless, the bleeding continued a while until it could be seen
with careful deliberation.

And this blood looked so plenteous that it seemed to me, if it had
been as plenteous in nature and in matter during that time,
it would have made the bed all bloody
and have overflowed around the outside.

And then it came to my mind that God has made plentiful waters on
earth for our assistance and for our bodily comfort because of the
tender love He has for us,
but it still pleases Him better if we accept most beneficially His
blessed blood to wash us from sin.
There is no liquid that is made
which it pleases Him so well to give us,
for just as it is most plentiful,
so it is most precious
(and that by the virtue of His blessed Godhead).

And the blood is of our own nature, and all beneficently flows over
us by the virtue of His precious love.

The dearworthy blood of our Lord Jesus Christ,
as truly as it is most precious,
so truly it is most plentiful.

Behold and see.

The precious abundance of His dearworthy Blood
descended down into hell,
and burst their bonds
and delivered all that were there
who belonged to the court of heaven.

The precious abundance of His dearworthy Blood
    flows over all earth
    and is quick to wash all creatures from sin who are of good will,
        have been, and shall be.

The precious abundance of His dearworthy Blood
    ascended up into heaven
    to the blessed Body of our Lord Jesus Christ,
    and there it is within Him,
        bleeding and praying for us to the Father—
    and it is and shall be so as long as it is needed.

And evermore it flows in all heavens
    rejoicing in the salvation of all mankind that are there
        and shall be,
    completing the count that falls short.

13

Afterwards,
    before God showed any words,
He permitted me to gaze on Him a suitable time—
    and on all that I had seen
    and all the comprehension that was in it
    (as much as the simplicity of the soul could receive it).

Then, without voice or an opening of lips, He formed in my soul these
    words:
    "With this the Fiend is overcome."

            (Our Lord said these words, referring to His Blessed
            Passion as He showed it before.)

In this our Lord showed that His Passion is the overcoming of the
    Fiend.

God showed that the Fiend
    has now the same malice that he had before the incarnation;
    and no matter how vigorously nor how constantly he labors,
        he sees that all salvation's souls escape him gloriously
            by virtue of Christ's precious Passion.

That is his sorrow, and most unpleasantly is he brought down,
      because all that God allows him to do
    brings us to joy
    and him to shame and woe and pain.

And he has as much sorrow
    when God gives him leave to work
      as when he does not work
        (and that is because he can never do as much evil as he
        would like, for his power is all locked in God's hand).

(But in God can be no wrath, as I see it,
    for our good Lord endlessly has regard for His own honor
    and for the benefit of all that shall be saved.)

With power and justice He withstands the Reprobate
    who because of malice and shrewdness
    busies himself to conspire and to act against God's will.

Also I saw our Lord scorn the Fiend's malice
    and totally discount his powerlessness
        (and He wills that we do so, too).

Because of this sight I laughed mightily,
    and that made them laugh that were about me,
    and their laughing was a delight to me.
I thought that I wished that all my fellow Christians had seen as I
had seen,
    and then would they all laugh with me.

(Except I saw not Christ laughing; even though I was well aware that it was the sight that He showed which made me laugh, because I understood that we can laugh in comforting ourselves and rejoicing in God, because the Devil is overcome. And when I saw Him scorn the Devil's malice, it was only by a leading of my understanding into our Lord, that is to say, an inward showing of constancy, without alteration of outward expression for, as I see it, constancy is a worthy quality that is in God, which is enduring.)

After this I fell into a soberness and said:
"I see three things: amusement, scorn, and seriousness.

I see amusement in that the Fiend is overcome.

I see scorn in that God scorns him and he shall be scorned.

And I see seriousness in that he is overcome by the blissful Passion and Death of our Lord Jesus Christ which was done in full earnest and with weary labor."

(When I said, "He is scorned," I mean that God scorns him—that is to say: because He sees him now as He shall see him without end.)

In this God showed that the Fiend is damned
(and this I meant when I said, "He shall be scorned":
at Doomsday generally by all who shall be saved—
for whose salvation he has great envy).
Then he shall see that all the woe and tribulation that he has done to them shall be turned into increase of their joy without end, and all the pain and tribulation to which he would have brought them, shall endlessly go with him to hell.

14

After this our good Lord said:
"I thank thee for thy labor and especially for thy youth."

And in this showing my understanding was lifted up into heaven where I saw our Lord as a lord in his own house, who has called all his dearworthy servants and friends to a solemn feast. Then I saw the lord take no special high-ranked seat in his own household, but I saw him royally reign throughout his house, and he filled it full of joy and mirth himself, in order endlessly to cheer and comfort his dearworthy friends most plainly and most graciously, with marvelous melody of endless love in his own fair blessed face (which glorious face of the Godhead fills up heavens of joy and bliss).

God showed three degrees of bliss that every soul shall have in heaven who has willingly served God in any degree on earth.

The first is the honor-filled favor of our Lord God which the soul shall receive when it is delivered from pain.

This favor is so exalted and so full of honor that it seems to the soul that it fills him completely even if there were nothing more, for it seemed to me that all the pain and labor that could be suffered by all living men could not deserve the honorable gratitude that one man shall have who has willingly served God.

The second, that all the blessed creatures that are in heaven shall see that honorable favor, and He makes that man's service known to all that are in heaven.

And at this time, this example was shown: a king, if he thanks his servants, it is a great honor to them, and if he makes it known to all the realm, then is the servant's honor much increased.

The third is that as new and as pleasing as it is to receive it at that moment, just so shall it last without end.

And I saw that simply and sweetly was this shown: that the age of every man shall be known in heaven, and shall be rewarded for his willing service and for his time; and especially is the age of those who willingly and freely offer their youth to God excellently rewarded and wonderfully thanked.

For I saw that whenever or at whatever time a man or woman is
truly turned to God,
for one day's service and in order to fulfill His endless will,
that one shall enjoy all these three degrees of bliss.

And the more that the loving soul sees this graciousness of God,
the more it prefers to serve Him all the days of its life.

15

After this He showed a most excellent spiritual pleasure in my soul:
I was completely filled with everlasting certainty,
powerfully sustained without any painful fear.
This feeling was so joyful and so spiritual that I was wholly in
peace and in repose and there was nothing on earth that would
have grieved me.

This lasted only a while, and I was changed
and left to myself in such sadness and weariness of my life, and
annoyance with myself that scarcely was I able to have patience
to live. There was no comfort nor any ease for me except faith,
hope, and love, and these I held in truth (but very little in feeling).

And immediately after this, our Blessed Lord gave me again the
comfort and the rest in my soul,
in delight and in security so blissful and so powerful
that no fear, no sorrow, no bodily pain that could be suffered
would have distressed me.

And then the pain showed again to my feeling,

and then the joy and the delight,

and now the one,
and now the other,
various times—I suppose about twenty times.

And in the times of joy, I could have said with Saint Paul:
    "Nothing shall separate me from the love of Christ."
And in the pain I could have said with Peter:
    "Lord, save me, I perish."

This vision was shown me, for my understanding,
    that it is advantageous for some souls to feel this way—
sometime to be in comfort,
and sometimes to fail and to be left by themselves.

God wants us to know that He protects us equally surely in woe and
    in well.

But for the benefit of man's soul a man is sometimes left to himself
    (although sin is not always the cause—for during this time I
        committed no sin for which I should be left to myself, for it
        was so sudden).
(Equally, I deserved not to have this blessed feeling.)

But freely our Lord gives when He wishes,
    and permits us to be in woe sometimes.

And both are one love,
    for it is God's will that we keep us in this comfort with all our
        might,
    because bliss is lasting without end,
    and pain is passing and shall be brought to nothing for those who
        shall be saved.

And therefore it is not God's will
    that we submit to the feeling of pains, in sorrow and mourning
        because of them,
    but quickly pass over them and keep ourselves in the endless
        delight which is God.

16

After this Christ showed a portion of His Passion near His death.
  I saw His sweet face
    and it was dry and bloodless with pale dying and deathly ashen;
    and after that more pale, grievous, distressing,
    and then turned more lifeless into blue,
    and after that more brown-blue, as the flesh changed into more
      profound death.

His suffering revealed itself to me most distinctly in His blessed face,
  and especially in His lips where I saw these four colors
  (though before those lips were fresh, ruddy, and pleasant to my
    sight).

This was a sorrowful change to see this profound dying,
  and also the nose was shrivelled together and dried, as I saw it,
  and the sweet body became brown and black,
  all changed from the fair life-like color of Himself into dry dying;
    because at the time that our Lord and Blessed Savior died
    upon the rood, there was a dry, sharp wind and wondrous
    cold, as I see it.

And by the time all the Precious Blood was bled out of the sweet
    body that could pass from it,
  yet there remained a moisture in the sweet flesh of Christ,
    as it was shown.

Bloodlessness and painful drying within
and the blowing of wind and cold coming from without
met together in the sweet body of Christ.

And these four,
  two without,
  and two within,
dried the flesh of Christ over the course of time.

And though this pain was bitter and sharp,
    it was most long-lasting, as I saw it,
    and it painfully dried up all the living elements of Christ's Flesh.

Thus I saw the sweet Flesh die,
    apparently part after part,
    drying with awesome pains.

And as long as any element had life in Christ's flesh,
    so long He suffered pain.

This long torment seemed to me as if He had been seven nights
        lifeless,
    dying,
    at the point of passing away,
    suffering the last pain.
        (And when I say it seemed to me as if He had been seven nights
        lifeless, it means that the sweet body was as discolored, as dry,
        as shrivelled, as deathlike and as piteous as though He had been
        seven nights lifeless, constantly dying.)

And it seemed to me that the drying of Christ's Flesh
        was the worst pain,
    and the last,
    of His Passion.

17

In this dying was brought to my mind the words of Christ: "I thirst,"
    for I saw in Christ a double thirst:
    one bodily,
    another spiritual
        (which I shall speak of in the thirty-first chapter).

I was reminded of this word
  because of the bodily thirst
    which I understood was caused by the lack of moisture,
    for the blessed flesh and bones were left all alone
    without blood and moisture.

The blessed body dried all alone a long time,
  with the twisting of the nails
  and weight of the body
    (for I understood that because of the tenderness of the sweet
      hands and of the sweet feet, and by the large size, cruelty,
      and hardship of the nails, the wounds grew wider),
  and the body sagged because of the weight by hanging a long time
  and the piercing and wrenching of the head
  and the binding of the crown,
    all parched with dry blood,
      with the sweet hair and the dry flesh clinging to the thorns,
      and the thorns to the drying flesh.
And in the beginning
    while the flesh was fresh and bleeding,
  the constant settling of the thorns made the wounds wide.

Furthermore I saw that the sweet skin and the tender flesh,
  with the hair and the blood,
    were all raised and loosened above from the bone with the
      thorns,
    and gashed in many pieces,
    and were hanging like a cloth that was sagging as if it would
      very soon have fallen off because of the weight and loose-
      ness while it had natural moisture.
    (And that was great sorrow and fear for me, because it
      seemed to me that I would not for my life have seen it fall.)

How it was done, I saw not, but understood it was with the sharp
thorns and the violent and painful setting on of the garland
unsparingly and without pity.

This continued a while, and soon it began to change,
and I beheld and wondered how it could be.

And then I saw it was because the flesh began to dry
and lose a part of the weight that was round about the garland.
With this it was surrounded all about, as it were garland upon
garland.
The garland of the thorns was dyed with the blood, and the other
fleshly garland and the head were also the same color—
like clotted blood when it is dry.

The skin of the flesh of the face and of the body which showed
had small wrinkles,
with a tanned color,
like a dry board when it is old,
and the face was more brown than the body.

I saw four kinds of dryings:
the first was bloodless;
the second was pain following after;
the third was that He was hanging up in the air the way men hang
a cloth to dry;
the fourth, that His bodily nature demanded fluid and there was no
kind of comfort administered to Him in all His woe and
distress.

Ah! cruel and grievous was His pain,
but much more cruel and grievous it was
when the moisture was lacking and all began to dry,
shrivelling this way.

These were two pains that showed in the blessed head:
the first caused the drying while it was moist;
and the other slow, with shrivelling and drying, with blowing of
the wind from without that dried Him and pained Him more
with cold, more than my heart can think.

And all the other pains, because of which I saw that all I can say is
   too little, for it cannot be told!

That showing of Christ's pains filled me full of pain,
   because I was well-aware that He suffered only once,
   though He wished to show it me,
   and fill me with awareness as I had before desired.

And in all this time of Christ's pains
      I felt no pain except for Christ's pains.
   Then I thought, "I knew but little what pain it was
         that I asked for,"
      and like a wretch I repented me,
      thinking that if I had known what it would be,
      I would have been loath to have prayed for it,
      for it seemed to me that my pains went beyond any bodily death.

I thought: "Is any pain in hell like this?"
   And I was answered in my reason:
      "Hell is a different pain, for there is despair.
      But of all pains that lead to salvation,
      this is the most pain—
         to see thy Beloved suffer."

How can any pain be more to me than to see Him who is all my life,
all my bliss, and all my joy, suffer?

Here I felt most truthfully that I loved Christ so much more than
myself that there was no pain that could be suffered like to that
sorrow which I had to see Him in pain.

18

Here I saw a part of the compassion of Our Lady Saint Mary,
   for Christ and she were so one-ed in love
   that the magnitude of her love caused the magnitude of her pain.

In this I saw the essence of natural love, extended by grace, which
  creatures have for Him
and this natural love was most fulsomely shown
in His sweet Mother,

and even more,
  for in so much as she loved Him more than all others,
  her pains surpassed all others.

For ever the higher, the mightier, the sweeter that the love is,
  the more sorrow it is to the lover to see that body
  which is beloved in pain.

And all His disciples and all His true lovers suffered more pains than
their own bodily dying,
  for I am certain, by my own experience,
    that the least of them loved Him so far above himself that it
    surpasses all that I can say.

Here I saw a great one-ing between Christ and us, as I understand
  it, for when He was in pain, we were in pain.

And all created things that could suffer pain suffered with Him (that
  is to say, all created things that God has made for our service).
The firmament and the earth failed for sorrow in their nature at the
time of Christ's dying,
  for it belongs naturally to their character to know Him for their
  God in whom all their strength is situated.
    When He failed, then it was necessary for them out of nature to
    fail with Him as much as they could, out of sorrow for His pains.

And thus they that were His friends suffered pain for love.

And universally, all—that is to say, they that knew Him not—suffered
  because of the failing of all manner of comfort, except the
  mighty hidden protection of God.

45

I mean of two manner of folk, as it can be understood by two persons:
the one was Pilate,
the other was Saint Denis of France, who was at that time a
pagan;
for when he saw the wonders and marvels,
the sorrows and fears that happened at that time,
he said, "Either the world is now at an end,
or else He that is Maker of nature is suffering."
Wherefore, he did write on an altar: "This is the altar of the
unknown God."

God out of His goodness creates the planets and the elements in their
nature to work for both the blessed man and the cursed, and at that
time that goodness was withdrawn from both of them.

It was for that reason that even they who knew Him not were in
sorrow at that time.

Thus was our Lord Jesus given pain because of us,
and we all stand in this kind of pain with Him,
and shall do until we come to His bliss, as I shall say later.

19

At this time I wished to look up from the Cross,
and I dared not,
for I was well aware that while I gazed on the cross
I was secure and safe;
therefore I would not agree to put my soul in peril,
because, aside from the cross,
there was no protection from the horror of demons.

Then I had a proposal in my reason (as if it were like a friend) which
said to me, "Look up to heaven to His Father."

And I saw well with the Faith that there was nothing between the
cross and heaven that could have distressed me.
Either it was appropriate for me to look up, or else to answer.

I answered inwardly with all the powers of my soul and said,
"No, I cannot, for Thou art my heaven."
(This I said because I wished not to look up, for I had
rather have been in that pain until Doomsday than to have
come to heaven otherwise than by Him, for I was well-
aware that He who bound me so painfully, He would unbind
me when He wished.)

So was I taught to choose Jesus for my heaven, whom I saw only in
pain at that time.
I delighted in no other heaven than Jesus, who shall be my bliss
when I come there.

And this has ever been a comfort to me: that I chose Jesus for my
heaven, by His grace, in all this time of suffering and sorrow.
And that had been a learning for me that I should evermore do so,
choosing only Jesus for my heaven in well and woe.

And although like a sinner I had been sorry
(I said before that if I had been aware what pain it would be, I
would have been loath to have asked for it)
here saw I truly that it was the grouching and cursing of the flesh
without agreement of the soul
to which God assigns no blame.

Repenting and willing choice are two opposites which I experienced
both at once at the same time; and they are two parts:
the one outward,
the other inward.
The outward part is our mortal flesh which is now in pain and woe
(and always shall be in this life) of which I experienced much
at this time, and that was the part that repented.

47

The inward part is an exalted, blissful life which is totally in peace
and love, and this was more secretly experienced;
and this part is that in which mightily, wisely, and willingly,
I chose Jesus for my heaven.

And in this I saw truly that
the inward part is master and ruler of the outward,
and neither receives orders nor pays heed to the will of the
outward,
but its whole intention and will is endlessly committed to being
one-ed into our Lord Jesus.
(That the outward part could turn the inward to agreement
was not shown to me; but rather that the inward moves the
outward by grace, and both shall be united in bliss without
end by the power of Christ, this was shown.)

20

And thus I saw our Lord Jesus lingering a long time
[for the unity of the Godhead gave strength to the manhood out of
love to suffer more than all men could suffer].
(I mean not only more pain than all men could suffer, but also
that He suffered more pain than all men of salvation who ever
were from the first beginning until the last day, could measure
or fully imagine—considering the worthiness of the most exalted, honorable King and the shameful, spiteful, painful death—
because He that is most exalted and most worthy was most fully
brought to nothing and most utterly despised.)

The most significant point that can be seen in the Passion is to
comprehend and to understand
that He who suffered is *God*—
seeing beyond this two other points which are lesser
(the one is *what* He suffered,
and the other *for whom* He suffered).

In this showing He brought partially to mind
    the exaltation and nobility of the glorious Godhead,
    and with that the preciousness and the tenderness of the blessed
        body (which are both united together)
    and also the loathing that is in our nature to suffer pain;
        for as much as He was most tender and pure,
        just so He was most strong and mighty to suffer.

And for the sin of every man that shall be saved He suffered.
And because of every man's sorrow and desolation and anguish,
    He saw and grieved out of kindness and love.
      (In as much as Our Lady grieved for His pains,
        just so much He suffered grief for her sorrow, and more beyond,
           in as much as the sweet Manhood of Him was more noble
           in nature.)

As long as He was able to suffer,
    He suffered for us and grieved for us,
    and now He is risen and no more able to suffer,
        yet He suffers with us still (as I shall say later).

And I, gazing upon all this by His grace, saw that the love in Him
which He has for our soul was so strong that
    willingly He chose the Passion with great desire,
    and humbly He suffered it with great joy, with great satisfaction.

The soul that sees it in this way, when it is touched by grace, shall
truly see that the pains of Christ's Passion surpass all pains—that is
to say, those pains which shall be changed into everlasting surpassing
joys by the power of Christ's Passion.

21

It is God's will, as I understand it, that we have three ways of looking
    at His blessed Passion.

The first (which we should view with contrition and compassion)
is the cruel pain that He suffered; and that one our Lord
showed at this time and gave me power and grace to see it.

And I looked for the departing of His life with all my might and
expected to have seen the body entirely dead,
but I saw Him not so.

And just at the same time that I thought, by appearance,
that His life could no longer last,
and the showing of the end properly needed to be near,
suddenly, as I gazed upon the same cross,
He changed His blessed countenance.

The changing of His blessed countenance changed mine,
and I was as glad and as merry as possible.

Then brought Our Lord merrily to my mind:
"Where is now any point to thy pain or to thy distress?"
And I was completely happy.

I understood that, in our Lord's meaning,
we are now on His cross with Him
in our pains and our suffering, dying;
and if we willingly remain on the same cross with His help and His
grace until the last moment,
suddenly He shall change his appearance to us,
and we shall be with Him in heaven
(between the one and the other there shall be no passage
of time)
and then shall all be brought to joy.

And so meant He in this showing:
"Where is now any point to thy pain or thy distress?"
And we shall be fully blessed.

And here I saw truthfully that if He showed us His most blessed face
now, there is no pain on earth nor in any other place that would
distress us, but everything would be to us joy and bliss.
But because He showed to us an expression of suffering as He bore
in this life His cross,
therefore we are in distress and labor with Him as our frailty
demands.

And the reason why He suffers is because He wishes of His goodness
to make us heirs with Him in His bliss.

And for this little pain that we suffer here we shall have an exalted,
endless knowledge in God, which we could never have without that
pain.

The crueler our pains have been with Him on His cross, the more
shall our honor be with Him in His Kingdom.

22

Then spoke our good Lord Jesus Christ, asking:
   "Art thou well satisfied that I suffered for thee?"
I said: "Yea, good Lord, thanks be to Thee.
   Yea, good Lord, blessed mayest Thou be!"
Then said Jesus, our kind Lord:
   "If thou art satisfied, I am satisfied.
   It is a joy, a bliss, an endless delight to me that ever I suffered the
      Passion for thee;
   and if I could suffer more, I would suffer more."

In this experience my understanding was lifted up into heaven,
      and there I saw three states of bliss,
      by which sight I was greatly amazed.
   (And although I say "three states of bliss," if all are in the blessed

Manhood of Christ, no one is more, no one is less, no one is higher,
no one is lower, but equally alike in bliss.)

With respect to the first state,
    Christ showed me his Father
        (in no bodily likeness, but in His quality and in His actions—
        that is to say, I saw in Christ what the Father is).
    The action of the Father is this: that He gives recompense to
        His Son, Jesus Christ. This gift and this recompense is so
        blessed to Jesus that His Father could have given him no
        recompense that could have pleased Him better.
    The first state—that is, the pleasing of the Father—appeared to
        me as a heaven,
    and it was filled with bliss,
        for the Father is fully pleased with all the deeds that Jesus has
        done concerning our salvation.

    Wherefore, we are not only His by His paying for us,
        but also by the gracious gift of His Father
    we are His bliss;
    we are His recompense;
    we are His honor;
    we are His crown (and this was a particular wonder and a
        wholly delightful vision: that we are His crown).

This that I describe is such great bliss to Jesus that He sets at nought
    all His labor
    and His hard Passion
    and His cruel and shameful death.

And in these words:
    "If I could suffer more, I would suffer more,"
I saw truly that as often as He could die, so often He would,
and love would never let Him have rest until He had done it.

And I watched with great diligence in order to know how often He would die if He could,

> and truly, the number passed my understanding and my wits so far that my reason could not, nor knew how to, contain it or take it in.

And when He had thus often died (or was willing to),

> *still* He would set it at nought for love;
> for He considers everything but little in comparison to His love;
> for though the sweet Manhood of Christ could suffer but once, the goodness in Him can never cease from offering;
> every day He is prepared for the same, if it could be; for if He said He would for my love make new heavens and new earth, that were but little in comparison, for this could be done every day if He wished, without any labor;
> but to *die* for my love so often that the number passes created reason, that is the most exalted offer that our Lord God could make to man's soul, as I see it.

Then He means this:

> "How could it then be that I would not do for thy love all that I could?—this deed does not distress me since I would for thy love die so often with no regard to my cruel pains."

And here I saw with respect to the second vision in this blessed Passion that the love that made Him suffer surpassed all His pains as far as Heaven is above earth;

> for the *pain* was a noble, honorable deed
> done at one time
> by the action of love;
> but the *love* was without beginning,
> is now,
> and shall be without ending.

> It was because of this love He said most sweetly these words: "If I could suffer more, I would suffer more."

53

He said not, "If it were *necessary* to suffer more . . ." for even though it were not necessary, if He could suffer more, He would.

This deed and action concerning our salvation was prepared as well as God could prepare it.

And here I saw a complete bliss in Christ;
> for His bliss would not have been complete if it could have been done any better.

23

In these three words: "It is a joy, a bliss, and endless delight to me" were shown three states of bliss, in this way:
> in regard to the joy, I interpret the pleasure of the Father; and
> in regard to the bliss, the honor of the Son; and
> in regard to the endless delight, the Holy Spirit.

The Father is pleased,
the Son is honored,
the Holy Spirit delights.

> And here I saw this in relation to the third vision of His blessed Passion—that is to say, the joy and the bliss that make Him delight in it—for our gracious Lord showed His Passion to me in five ways: of which

>> the first is the bleeding of the head,
>> the second is the discoloring of His blessed face,
>> the third is the plenteous bleeding of the body in the slashes of the scourging,
>> the fourth is the profound drying (these four regard the *pains* of the Passion as I said before), and,

the fifth is what was shown in regard to the joy and the
bliss of the Passion.

It is God's will that we have true delight with Him in our salvation,
and in that He wishes us to be mightily comforted and strengthened, and thus He wills that with His grace our soul be happily
engaged,
for we are His bliss,
for in us He delights without end and
so shall we in Him with His grace.

All that He has done for us, and does now, and ever shall do,
was never a cost or burden to Him,
nor can it be
(except only what He did in our manhood, beginning at the
sweet incarnation and lasting until the blessed Rising on Easter
morning—only that long did the cost and the burden concerning
our redemption last in deed—about which deed He rejoices
endlessly, as was said before.)

Ah, Jesus wishes
that we take heed to the bliss of our salvation that is in the blessed
Trinity and
that we desire to have as much spiritual pleasure, with His grace,
as was said before.
(That is to say, that the pleasure of our salvation be like to the
joy that Christ has about our salvation as much as it can be while
we are here.)

The whole Trinity acted in the Passion of Christ
(ministering an abundance of strengths and plenitude of grace
to us by Him)
but only the Maiden's son suffered
(about which the whole blessed Trinity endlessly rejoices).

This was shown in these words: "Art thou well satisfied?"
and by that other word that Christ said, "If thou art satisfied, then I am satisfied"
(as if He said: "It is joy and delight enough to me, and I ask nothing else from thee for my labor except that I can well satisfy thee").

In this He reminded me of the quality of a glad giver:
always a glad giver takes but little heed of the thing that he gives,
but all his desire and all his intention is to please him and solace him to whom he gives it,
and if the receiver accepts the gift gladly and thankfully, then the gracious giver sets at nought all his cost and all his labor for the joy and delight that he has because he has pleased and solaced him whom he loves.
Plenteously and fully was this shown.

Think also wisely of the magnitude of this word "ever";
for in that was shown an exalted awareness of the love that He has in our salvation,
with the manifold joys that result from the Passion of Christ:
one joy is that He rejoices that He has done it in deed, and He shall suffer no more;
another joy is that He brought us up into heaven and made us to be His crown and endless bliss;
another joy is that with the Passion He has redeemed us from endless pains of hell.

24

Then, with a glad expression, our Lord looked into His wounded side and gazed with joy,
and with His sweet gazing He directed the understanding of His creature through that same wound into His side within.

56

There He showed a fair, desirable place, and large enough for all
 mankind
that shall be saved to rest in peace and love.
And with that He brought to mind His dearworthy blood and
 precious water which He allowed to pour all out for love.

And with the sweet sight He showed His blessed Heart
 cloven in two.
And with this sweet rejoicing, He showed to my understanding, in
 part, the blessed Godhead, strengthening the pure soul to
 understand (in so far as it can be expressed)
that this Heart is to signify the endless love that was without
 beginning, and is, and shall be always.

With this our Good Lord said most blissfully, "Lo, how I love thee"
 (as if He had said:
 "My dear one, behold and see the Lord, thy God,
 who is thy Creator and thine endless Joy.
 See thine own Brother, thy Savior;
 my child, behold and see what delight and bliss
 I have in thy salvation,
 and for my love, enjoy it now with me.").

Also for further understanding this blessed word was said:
 "Lo, how I love thee.
 Behold and see that I loved thee so much before I died for thee
 that I was willing to die for thee;
 and that now I have died for thee, and suffered willingly
 what I can.
 And now is all my bitter pain and all my cruel labor changed to
 endless joy and bliss for me and for thee.
 How should it now be that thou wouldst pray for anything that
 pleases me, and I would not most gladly grant it thee?
 For my pleasure is thy holiness and thine endless joy and bliss
 with Me."

This is the understanding, as simply as I can express it, of this blessed
  word: "Lo, how I love thee."

This our good Lord showed in order to make us glad and happy.

25

With this same expression of mirth and joy,
  our good Lord looked down on His right side
  and brought to my mind where Our Lady stood
  at the time of His Passion;
    and He said, "Dost thou wish to see her?"
      (And in this sweet word, it was as if He had said:
      "I know well thou wouldest see my Blessed Mother,
      for after Myself, she is the highest joy that I could show thee,
      and the most pleasure and honor to me;
      and she is most desired to be seen
      by all my blessed creatures.")

Because of the exalted, wondrous, special love that He has for this
sweet Maiden, His Blessed Mother, our Lady Saint Mary,
  He showed her highly rejoicing
    (as in view of the intention of these sweet words)
  as if He said:
    "Dost thou wish to see how I love her,
    that thou canst rejoice with me in the love that I have in her and
    she in me?"

And also for further understanding, this sweet word our Lord God
speaks to all mankind that shall be saved (as it were all to one
person) as if He said:
  "Do you wish to see in her how thou art loved?
  Because of thy love I made her so exalted, so noble, and so worthy;
  and this pleases me, and so I wish that it pleaseth thee."

For after Himself, she is the most blessed sight.

> (But from this I am not taught to yearn to see her bodily
> presence while I am here, but the virtues of her blessed
> soul—her truth, her wisdom, her love—whereby I can learn
> to know myself and reverently fear my God.)

And when our Good Lord had shown this and said this word,
"Dost thou wish to see her?"
I answered and said: "Yea, good Lord, thanks be to Thee;
yea, good Lord, if it be Thy will."

Often I prayed this and I expected to have seen her in bodily
presence, but I saw her not so,
but Jesus in that word showed me a spiritual sight of her (in the
same way as I had seen her before—little and simple—so He
showed her now exalted and noble and glorious and pleasing
to Him above all created beings).

And so He wishes that it be known that all those that delight in Him
should delight in her and in the delight that He has in her and she in
Him.

For further understanding, He showed this example:
as, if a man loves a creature uniquely above all creatures,
he would like to make all creatures to love and to delight in that
creature which he loves so much.

And in this word that Jesus said, "Dost thou wish to see her?" it
seemed to me that it was the most pleasing word He could have
given me about her with the spiritual showing that He gave me of
her—because our Lord showed me no one person in particular except
our Lady Saint Mary—and her He showed three times:
the first was as she conceived,
the second was as she was in her sorrows beneath the cross,
the third was as she is now in delight, honor, and joy.

26

After this our Lord showed Himself more glorified, as I see it, than I
    saw Him before,
    in which I was taught that our soul shall never rest until it comes
    to Him
        knowing that He is the fullness of joy,
            simple and gracious,
            blissful and true life itself.
Our Lord Jesus often said:
    "It is I,
    it is I;
    it is I who am most exalted;
    it is I whom thou lovest;
    it is I whom thou enjoyest;
    it is I whom thou servest;
    it is I whom thou yearnst for;
    it is I whom thou desirest;
    it is I whom thou meanest;
    it is I who am all;
    it is I whom Holy Church preaches and teaches thee;
    it is I who showed myself here to thee."

The number of these words surpasses my wit and all my understanding and all my abilities, and it is a most high number, as I see it,
because therein is contained—I cannot count—but the joy that I saw
in the showing of these words surpasses all that heart can wish and
soul can desire. And therefore the words are not explained here, but
every man according to the grace that God gives him in interpreting
and loving, receive them in our Lord's meaning.

27

After that the Lord brought to my mind the yearning that I had for
Him in the past,

and I saw that nothing stood in my way except sin
  (and thus I observed universally in us all).

And it seemed to me that if sin had not been,
  we would all have been pure
  and like to our Lord as He made us,

and thus, in my folly, before this time I often wondered why, by the
great foreseeing wisdom of God,
the beginning of sin was not prevented,
  for then, it seemed to me, all would have been well.

I ought much to have given up this disturbing wondering, but nevertheless, I made mourning and sorrow about it without reason or
  discretion.

But Jesus (who in this vision informed me of all that I needed)
  answered by this word and said:
  "Sin is inevitable,
    but all shall be well,
    and all shall be well,
    and all manner of thing shall be well."

In this unadorned word "sin," our Lord brought to my mind generally
  all that is not good,
  and the shameful despising
  and the uttermost tribulation that He bore for us in this life,
  and His dying,
  and all the pains and sufferings of all His created things, spiritually
    and bodily
    (for we are all in part troubled—and we shall be troubled,
    following our Master Jesus, until we are completely purged—
    that is to say, until we are fully stripped of our mortal flesh and
    of all our inward affections which are not truly good).

61

And with the beholding of this,
    with all pains that ever were or ever shall be,
    I understood the Passion of Christ to represent the greatest pain
        and even more than that.

And all this pain was shown in one stroke
    and quickly passed over into comfort
        (for our good Lord does not wish that the soul be made fearful
        by this ugly sight).

But I saw not sin;
    for I believe it has no manner of essence
    nor any portion of being,
    nor can it be known except by the pain that is caused by it.
        And this pain, it is something for a time, as I see it, because it
        purges and forces us to know ourselves and ask for mercy. But
        the Passion of our Lord is comfort for us against all this, and so
        is His blessed will.

And because of the tender love that our good Lord has to all that
    shall be saved, He comforts quickly and sweetly, meaning thus:
    "It is true that sin is cause of all this pain,
        but all shall be well,
        and all shall be well,
        and all manner of thing shall be well."

These words were said most tenderly,
    showing no manner of blame to me nor to any that shall be saved.

Then it would be a great unkindness to blame and question God for
    my sin, seeing He does not blame me for sin.

In these same words I saw a marvelous, high secret hidden in God,
    which secret He shall openly make known to us in heaven.

In this secret knowledge we shall truly see the reason why He
   allowed sin to come,
   and in this sight we shall endlessly rejoice in our Lord God.

28

Thus I saw how Christ has compassion for us because of sin.

And just as
   I was before filled with pain and compassion
      for the Passion of Christ, similarly,
   I was here filled in part with compassion for all my fellow
      Christians for that is to say
      (even though He full well loves the people that shall be saved),
   that God's servants, Holy Church, shall be shaken in sorrows and
      anguish and tribulation in this world as men shake a cloth in
      the wind.

And regarding this our Lord answered in this manner:
      "A great thing shall I make out of this in heaven,
      of endless honors, and everlasting joys."

Yea, so much so that I saw that our Lord rejoices at the tribulations
of His servants (with pity and compassion),
   and upon each person whom He loves (in order to bring him to His
   bliss) He lays upon them something that is no defect from His
   point of view, whereby they are
      disparaged and despised in this world,
      scorned and mocked,
      and cast out.
   This He does in order to prevent the harm that they would receive
      from the pomp and
      from the pride and
      from the vainglory of this wretched life,

and to make their way ready to come to heaven,
and to exalt them in His bliss everlasting without end.

For He says:
"I shall totally shatter you because of your vain affections and
your vicious pride;
and after that I shall gather you together and make you humble
and gentle, pure and holy, by one-ing you to myself."

Then I saw
that each kind compassion that man has toward his fellow Christian
with love, it is Christ in him;
that each kind of degradation that He was shown in His Passion,
it was shown again here in this compassion in which there
were two kinds of applications of our Lord's meaning:
the one was the bliss that we are brought to in which
He wants us to rejoice;
the other is for comfort in our pain,
because He wants us to be aware that the pain shall all be
transformed into honor and benefit by virtue of His
Passion,
and that we be aware that we do not suffer alone, but with
Him,
and that we see Him as our foundation,
and that we see His pains and His tribulation surpass so far
all that we can suffer that it cannot be fully
comprehended.

And the careful awareness to this intention of His, saves us from
grumbling and despair when we experience our own pains
as long as we see truly that our sin deserves it,
yet His love excuses us,
and of His great graciousness He does away with all our blame,
and He looks upon us with mercy and pity as children,
innocent and not loathsome.

64

29

But in this showing I remained watching generally,
   sorrowful and mourning,
      saying thus to our Lord in my meaning with full great fear:
         "Ah! Good Lord, how can all be well considering the great
         damage that has come by sin to Thy creatures?"
            (And here I desired, as much as I dared, to have some more
            open explanation with which I could be put at ease
            in this matter.)

To this our blessed Lord answered most gently,
   and with most loving expression,
      and showed that Adam's sin was the most harm that ever was
         done, or ever shall be done, until the world's end
         (and also He showed that this is openly acknowledged in all the
         Holy Church on earth).

Furthermore, He taught that I should observe the glorious
   reparation, for making this reparation is more pleasing to the
   blessed Godhead and more valuable for man's salvation, without
   comparison, than ever was the sin of Adam harmful.

Then means our blessed Lord thus in this teaching: that we would
   take heed to this:
      "For since I had made well the *worst* harm,
      then it is my will that thou knowest from that
      that I shall make well everything that is *less* bad."

30

He gave me understanding in two parts:

   The first part is our Savior and our salvation;
      this blessed part is open and clear and fair and light and

plenteous, for all mankind that is of good will and shall be is contained in this part;
to this we are bound by God
and attracted and advised, and taught inwardly by the Holy Spirit and outwardly by Holy Church in the same grace;
in this our Lord wishes us to be engaged, rejoicing in Him because He rejoices in us, and
the more abundantly we accept this with reverence and humility, the more favor we earn from Him and
the more help for ourselves; and thus, we can see and rejoice that our portion is our Lord.

The second part is hidden and sealed from us
(that is to say, all except for our salvation),
for that is our Lord's secret purpose,
and it is proper to the royal authority of God to hold His secret purpose in peace,
and it is proper for His servants, out of obedience and reverence, not to wish to know His purpose.

Our Lord has pity and compassion on us because some creatures make themselves so busy about His secrets; and I am certain if we were aware of how much we would please Him and ease ourselves by abandoning that, we would.

The saints that are in heaven wish to know nothing except what our Lord wishes to show them,
and also their love and their desire is ruled according to the will of our Lord.
Thus we ought to wish as they do—then shall we not wish nor desire anything except the will of our Lord just as they do, for we are all one in God's purpose.

And here was I taught that we should trust and rejoice only in our blessed Savior Jesus, for everything.

31

And so our good Lord replied to all the questions and doubts that I
could raise,
saying most reassuringly:
"I am able to make everything well, and
I know how to make everything well, and
I wish to make everything well, and
I shall make everything well; and
thou shalt see for thyself that all manner of thing shall be well."

Where He says, "I am able," I understand as referring to the Father;
and
where He says, "I know how," I understand as referring to the Son;
and
where He says, "I wish to," I understand as referring to the Holy
Spirit; and
where He says, "I shall," I understand as referring to the unity of
the blessed Trinity (three persons and one truth); and
where He says, "Thou shalt see for thyself," I understand the one-
ing of all mankind that shall be saved into the blissful Trinity.

With these five words God wills that we be enclosed in rest and in
peace; and thus shall the spiritual thirst of Christ have an end,
for this is the spiritual thirst of Christ: the love-longing that lasts
and ever shall, until we see that sight on Doomsday.

[For of us who shall be saved, and shall be Christ's joy and His bliss,
some are still here, and some are to come (and so shall some be until
that Day).]

Therefore, this is His thirst:
a love-longing to possess us all together wholly within Himself for
His bliss, as I see it

(for we are not now fully as wholly within Him
as we shall be then).

For we know in our Faith
(and also it was shown in all the revelations)
that Christ Jesus is both God and man.

Concerning the Godhead, He is Himself highest bliss,
and was so from without beginning,
and shall be until without end;
this endless bliss can never be increased nor decreased in itself.
(This was plenteously seen in every showing—
and specifically in the twelfth where He says:
"It is I who am highest.")

Concerning Christ's manhood,
it is known in our Faith, and also shown in the revelation, that
He, with the strength of Godhead, for the sake of love,
endured pains and sufferings and died in order to bring us to
His bliss.
And these are the works of Christ's manhood, in which He
rejoices
(and that He showed in the ninth revelation where He says:
"It is a joy, a bliss, an endless delight to me that ever I
suffered the Passion for thee").
And this is the joy of Christ's works and this He means where
He said in the same showing that
we are His joy,
we are His recompense,
we are His honor,
we are His crown.

Concerning Christ as our *Head,*
He is glorified and beyond suffering, but concerning His
Body (in which His members are knit),
He is not yet fully glorified nor all beyond suffering; be-

68

cause the same desire and thirst which He had upon
the cross
(which desire, longing, and thirst, as I see it, was in Him
from without beginning),
the same desire and thirst has He still,
and shall have until the time that the last soul that shall be
saved has come up to His bliss.

For as truly as there is a quality in God of compassion and pity, just
as truly there is a quality in God of thirst and yearning.
And because of the strength of this yearning in Christ, we must
yearn also for Him (without which yearning, no soul comes to
heaven).

This quality of yearning and thirst comes from the endless goodness
of God (just as the quality of pity also comes from His goodness)
and even though He has both yearning and pity, they are two
different qualities, as I see it.
In this goodness is based the essence of the spiritual thirst, which
lasts in Him as long as we are in need, drawing us up to His
bliss.

(All this was seen in the showing forth of His compassion, for
that shall cease on Doomsday.)

Thus He has pity and compassion on us,
and He has a yearning to possess us,
but His wisdom and His love do not permit the end to come
until the best possible time.

32

One time our good Lord said: "All manner of thing shall be well";
and another time He said: "Thou shalt see for thyself that all manner
of thing shall be well";
and from these two words the soul received various applications.

One was this: that He wishes us to be aware that not only does
    He take heed to noble and to great things, but also to little
    and small things, to lowly and simple things,
  both to one and to the other;
  and so means He in that He says
    "All manner of thing shall be well";
  for He wills that we be aware that the least little thing shall
  not be forgotten.

Another understanding is this: that, from our point of view,
    there are many deeds evilly done and such great harm given
    that it seems to us that it would be impossible
    that ever it should come to a good end;
  and we look upon this,
  sorrowing and mourning because of it,
  so that we cannot take our ease in the joyful beholding of God
  as we would like to do;
    and the cause is this: that the use of our reason is now so
        blind, so lowly, and so stupid that we cannot know the
        exalted, wondrous Wisdom, the Power, and the Good-
        ness of the blessed Trinity;
  and this is what He means when He says,
    "Thou shalt see for thyself that all manner of thing
    shall be well,"
  as if He said,
    "Pay attention to this now, faithfully and trustingly, and at
    the last end thou shalt see it in fullness of joy."

And thus, in these same previous five words:
    "I am able to make everything well, etc.,"
  I interpret a mighty comfort about all the works of our Lord
    God that are still to come.

There is a Deed which the blessed Trinity shall do on the Last Day,
as I see it, and what the Deed shall be, and how it shall be done, is

70

unknown to all creatures that are beneath Christ, and shall remain so until when it is done.

The Goodness and the Love of our Lord God wills that we be aware that it *shall* be done, but His Power and Wisdom by the same Love wishes to keep and hide from us *what* it shall be and *how* it shall be done.

(And the reason why He wills that we know it in this way is because He wishes us to be more at ease in our soul and more peaceful in love, refraining from paying attention to all temptations that could obstruct us from truth, and rejoicing in Him.)

This is the Great Deed
> intended by our Lord God from without beginning,
> treasured and hidden in His blessed breast,
> known only to Himself,
by which Deed He shall make all things well.

For as the blessed Trinity created all things from nothing, just so the same blessed Trinity shall make well all that is not well.

At this sight I marveled greatly, and looked at our Faith, marveling thus: our Faith is based in God's word, and it is part of our Faith that we believe that God's word shall be preserved in all things,

and one point of our Faith is that many creatures shall be damned (as were the angels who fell out of heaven because of pride— who are now demons),

and many on earth who die outside of the Faith of Holy Church (that is to say, those who are heathen men and also men who have received Christianity but live unChristian lives and so die without love)

all these shall be damned to hell without end, as Holy Church teaches me to believe.

Given all this, it seemed to me that it was impossible that all manner of thing would be well as our Lord showed at this time;

71

and in regard to this, I had no other answer in any showing of our Lord God except this:

"What is impossible for thee is not impossible for me.
I shall preserve my word in all things,
and I shall make everything well."

Thus I was taught by the grace of God that I should steadfastly keep myself in the Faith as I had interpreted it before, and *also* that I should firmly believe that everything shall be well as our Lord showed at the same time; because this is the Great Deed that our Lord shall do, in which Deed He shall preserve His word in everything and He shall make well all that is not well.

But what the Deed shall be, and how it shall be done, there is no creature beneath Christ that either knows it or shall know it until it is done

(according to the understanding that I received of our Lord's meaning at this time).

33

And still in this showing I desired, as far as I dared, that I might have had full view of hell and purgatory.

(But it was not my intention to undertake to challenge anything that is part of the Faith—for I believe truthfully that hell and purgatory are for the same purpose that Holy Church teaches— but my intention was that for the sake of learning I might have seen everything that is part of my Faith, whereby I could live more to God's honor and to my benefit.)

But in spite of my desire I learned nothing whatsoever about this (except as it was said before in the fifth showing where I saw that the Devil was reproached by God and endlessly damned, in which showing I interpreted that all creatures that are of the Devil's character in this life and who end that way, there is no more mention made of them before God and all His holy ones than of the Devil, notwithstanding that they are of mankind, whether they have been baptized or not).

Although the revelation of goodness was made in which little mention of evil was made,
> yet in it I was not drawn away from any point of Faith that Holy Church teaches me to believe.
>> I saw the Passion of Christ in various showings (in the second, in the fifth and in the eighth showings, as I said before)
>>> (where I had a partial experience of the sorrow of Our Lady and of His true friends who saw Him in pain, but I did not see as specially described in detail the Jews that did Him to death. Nevertheless, I knew in my Faith that they were accursed and damned without end—except for those that were converted by grace).

I was strengthened and taught without exception
> to keep myself in every detail in the Faith,
> and in all that I had understood before,
> hoping that I was in that Faith with the mercy
>> and the grace of God,
> desiring and praying in my intentions that I might continue therein until my life's end.

It is God's will that we have great regard for all His deeds that He has done,
> for He wills thereby that we know, trust, and believe all that He shall do,
> and evermore it is necessary for us to leave off involving ourselves with what the Deed shall be,
> and desire to be like our brethren who are the saints in heaven who wish absolutely nothing but God's will,
> then shall we rejoice only in God and be well satisfied both with His hiding and with His showing,

for I saw truly in our Lord's meaning that the more we busy ourselves to know His secrets in this or any other thing, the farther shall we be from the knowledge of them.

34

Our Lord God showed two kinds of secrecies:
> one is the Great Secret with all the secret details that are part of it, and these things He wills that we understand are hidden until the time that He will clearly show them to us;
> the other are the secrets which He Himself showed openly in this revelation,
> > for they are secrets that He wishes to make open and known to us;
> > for He wants us to be aware that it is His will that we know them.
> > They are secrets to us not only because He wills they be secrets to us,
> > > but they are secrets to us because of our blindness and our ignorance.
> > > Concerning those weaknesses He has great pity, and therefore He wishes to make the secrets more open to us Himself, by which we can know Him and love Him and cleave to Him.

For all that is advantageous for us to be aware of and to know, full graciously our good Lord will show us through all the preaching and teaching of Holy Church.

God showed the very great pleasure that He has in all men and women who strongly and humbly and willingly receive
the preaching and teaching of Holy Church,
> for He *is* Holy Church—
> > He is the foundation,

He is the essence,
He is the teaching,
He is the teacher,
He is the goal,
He is the reward for which every natural soul toils.

And this is known and shall be known to every soul to which the Holy
Spirit declares it.

And I hope truly that He will assist all those who seek in this way,
for they seek God.

All this that I have said now, and more that I shall say later, is
reassuring against sin;
for in the third showing when I saw that God does all that is
done, I saw no sin,
and then I saw that all is well.
But when God showed me as regards sin,
then He said: "All shall be well."

35

When God Almighty had shown so plentifully and so fully of His
goodness, I desired to know of a certain creature that I loved if
it would continue in good living (which I hoped by the grace of
God was begun).
And in this particular desire, it seemed that I hindered myself,
because I was not shown at this time.

And then I was answered in my reason, as it were by a friendly
go-between:
"Take this generally, and see the graciousness of the Lord God
as He reveals it to thee; for it is more honor to God for thee to
see Him in all things than in any special thing."

I agreed, and with that I learned that it is more honor to God to
understand all things in general than to delight
in anything in particular.

And if I would do wisely following this teaching,
not only would I be glad for nothing in particular,
but also not greatly disturbed by any manner of thing,
for "All shall be well."

The fullness of joy is to behold God in all.

For by the same blessed Power, Wisdom, and Love by which He
created all things,
to the same end our good Lord leads those things constantly,
and thereto shall He Himself bring them,
and when it is time, we shall see it.

(The basis of this was shown in the first showing and more
openly in the third where it says, "I saw God in a point.")

All that our Lord does is rightful,
what he tolerates is honorable,
and in these two is included both good and evil.

All that is good our Lord does,
and what is evil our Lord tolerates.
(I say not that any evil is honorable,
but I say the *toleration* of our Lord God is honorable,
whereby His goodness shall be known without end in His
marvelous humility and gentleness,
by the action of mercy and grace.)

Rightfulness is that thing which is so good
that it cannot be better than it is,

for God Himself is true rightfulness,
and all His works are done rightfully as they are appointed from
without beginning
by His high Power,
His high Wisdom,
His high Goodness.

And just as He ordained all for the best,
just so He works constantly and leads it to that same end; and He is
ever most pleased with Himself and with His works.

The beholding of this blissful agreement is most sweet to the soul
that sees by grace.
All the souls that shall be saved in heaven without end are created
rightful in the sight of God, and by His own goodness,
and in this rightfulness we are endlessly and marvelously
preserved, more than all other created things.

Mercy is an action that comes from the goodness of God,
and it shall remain in action as long as sin is permitted to pursue
rightful souls,
and when sin has no longer permission to pursue,
then shall the action of mercy cease.
And then shall all be brought to rightfulness and remain therein
without end.

By His toleration, we fall,
and in His blessed Love with His Power and His Wisdom
we are preserved,
and by mercy and grace we are raised to many more joys.

And thus in rightfulness and in mercy He wishes to be known and
loved now without end. And the soul that wisely holds on to this in
grace, is well pleased with both, and endlessly rejoices.

36

Our Lord God showed me that a deed shall be done
  and He Himself shall do it;
  and it shall be honorable and marvelous and fruitful,
  and through me it shall be done,
  and He Himself shall do it.

And this is the highest joy that the soul recognized:
  that God Himself shall do it,
  and I shall do nothing at all except sin,
  and my sin shall not hinder His goodness from working.

And I saw that the beholding of this is an heavenly joy in a reverent soul which evermore naturally by grace desires God's will.

This deed shall be begun here,
and it shall be honorable to God
and plentifully beneficial to His lovers on earth,
and ever as we come to heaven we shall see it in marvelous joy,
and it shall last thus in operation until the Last Day,
and the honor and the bliss of it shall continue in heaven before God
    and all His holy ones without end.

In this way was this deed seen and interpreted in our Lord's
    intention,
  and the reason why He showed it
  is to cause us to rejoice in Him and all His works.

When I saw His showing continued, I understood that it was shown as a great event which was to come (which God showed that He Himself would do). This deed has these qualities which I mentioned before. This He showed most blissfully, intending that I should accept it wisely, faithfully, and trustingly.

But what this deed would be, that was kept secret from me.
And in this I saw that He wills not that we fear to know the things that He shows—
He shows them because He wishes us to know them and by this knowledge He wills that we love Him
and delight in Him
and endlessly rejoice in Him.

Because of the great love that He has for us,
He shows us all that is honorable and beneficial for the present.
The things that He wills to have secret now, still of His great goodness,
He shows them concealed,
in which showing He wills that we believe and recognize that we shall see them truly in His endless bliss.

Then we ought to rejoice in Him both for all that He shows,
and for all that He hides;
and if we willingly and humbly do this,
we shall find therein great ease,
and we shall have endless favor from Him for that.

Thus is the interpretation of this word: that it shall be done through me (that is, the general man, that is to say, all that shall be saved).

It shall be honorable and marvelous and fruitful and God Himself shall do it.
And this shall be the highest joy that can be, to behold the deed that God Himself shall do,
and man shall do absolutely nothing except sin.

Then means our Lord God thus: as if He said:
"Behold and see.
Here thou hast cause for humility;

here thou hast cause for love;

here thou hast cause to know thyself;

here thou hast cause to rejoice in me; and because of my love, do
rejoice in me, for of all things, with that thou canst most
please me."

And as long as we are in this life, whenever we by our folly turn to
paying attention to the Reprobate, tenderly our Lord God touches us
and blessedly calls us, saying in our soul:

"Let me be all thy love, my dearworthy child. Occupy thyself with
me, for I am enough for thee, and rejoice in thy Savior and in thy
salvation."

And I am certain that this is our Lord's action in us.

The soul that is pierced with it by grace shall see it
and experience it.

And though it is so that this deed be truly understood for the general
man, yet it does not exclude the particular;

for what our good Lord wishes to do through His poor creatures,
is now unknown to me.

This deed and the other I mentioned before, they are not both one,
but two different ones.

However this deed shall be done sooner,
and that other one shall be when we come to heaven.

And to whom our Lord gives it, this deed can be known in part,
but the Great Deed mentioned before shall neither be
known in heaven nor earth until it is done.

Besides this, He gave special understanding and teaching about the
working of miracles, thus:

"It is known that I have done miracles here before, many and very
exalted and astounding, honorable and great;
and just as I have done in the past, so I do now constantly,
and shall do in the course of time."

It is known that before miracles come sorrow and anguish and
tribulation; and that is so that we would know our own
feebleness and our misfortune that we have fallen into by sin
in order to humble us,
and cause us to fear God,
crying for help and grace.

And great miracles come after that,
and they come from the exalted Power, Wisdom, and Goodness of
God,
showing His strength and the joys of heaven (in so far as that
can be in this passing life),
and that in order to strengthen our faith and to increase our
hope, in love.

For that reason it pleases Him to be known and honored in miracles.
Then He means thus: He wills that we be not carried overly low
because of sorrows and temptations that befall us, for it has ever
been this way before the coming of miracles.

37

God reminded me that I would sin;
and because of the delight that I had in gazing upon Him, I did not
pay heed quickly to that showing.

And our Lord most mercifully waited and gave me grace to listen.

(And this showing I received particularly to myself, but by all
the gracious comfort that follows, as you shall see, I was taught
to accept it on behalf of all my fellow Christians—all in general,
and nothing in particular.)

Though our Lord showed me that I would sin, by "me alone" is
meant "all."

81

And in this I perceived a gentle anxiety, and to this our Lord answered: "I keep thee full safely."

This word was said with more love and steadiness and spiritual protection than I know how or am able to tell.

As it was shown that I would sin,
in just the same way was the comfort shown—safety and protection for all fellow Christians.

What can make me love my fellow Christians more than to see in God that He loves all that shall be saved as if they were all one soul?
For in every soul that shall be saved is a divine will that never consented to sin nor ever shall;
just as there is a savage will in the lower part of man which can will no good,
so, too, there is a divine will in the higher part of man which will is so good that it can never will evil, but always good,

and because of that we are what He loves,
and endlessly we do what delights Him.

And this our Lord showed the completeness of love in which we stand in His sight—
yea, that He loves us now as well while we are here as He shall when we are there before His blessed face.

So because of the falling away from love on our part,
from *that* is all our difficulty.

38

Also God showed that sin shall not be shame, but honor to man—for just as for every sin there is a corresponding pain in reality, just so, for every sin, to the same soul is given a blessing by love.

Just as various sins are punished with various pains according to how grievous they are,

just so shall they be rewarded with different joys in heaven for their victories after the sins have been painful and sorrowful to the soul on earth.

For the soul that shall come to heaven is so precious to God and the place so honor-filled

that the goodness of God never permits the soul that shall finally come there to sin

unless those sinners of that sort are to be rewarded

and made known in Holy Church on earth

and also in heaven without end,

and blessedly made good by exceeding honors.

In this vision my understanding was lifted up into heaven;

and then God brought cheerfully to my mind

David and others in the Old Law with him without number,

and in the New Law He brought to my mind first

Mary Magdalen,

Peter and Paul,

and Thomas and Jude

and Saint John of Beverly

and others also without number

and how they are recognized in the Church on earth along with their sins,

and it is to them no shame, but all of the sins have been changed to honor.

Because of that our gracious Lord shows about sins

here in part

like what it is there in fullness,

for there the sign of sin is turned to honor.

In comfort to us because of his familiarity
   our Lord showed Saint John of Beverly,
      very exalted,
and brought to my mind how he is a neighbor at hand
         and of our acquaintance.
And God called him "Saint John of Beverly" as clearly as we do, and
      did so with a very glad, sweet expression showing that he is a
      most exalted saint in heaven in His sight, and a blessed one.

With this He made mention that in Saint John's youth and in his
tender time of life, he was a dearworthy servant of God, much loving
and fearing God,
   and nevertheless God allowed him to fall,
   mercifully protecting him so that he did not perish
   nor lose any time.

And afterward, God raised him to many times more grace,
   and by the contrition and humility that He showed in his living,
   God has given him in heaven manifold joys exceeding what he
      would have had if he had not fallen.

And God shows that this is true on earth by the working of plenteous
miracles around Saint John's body constantly.

And all this was to make us glad and cheerful in love.

39

Sin is the harshest scourge that any chosen soul can be struck with.
   This scourge chastises a man and woman terribly
   and damages him in his own eyes to such an extent that sometimes
      he thinks of himself as not worthy except to sink into hell—
   until contrition seizes him by the touching of the Holy Spirit
   and changes the bitterness into hopes for God's mercy.

Then his wounds begin to heal
  and the soul, directed into the life of Holy Church, begins to revive.
    The Holy Spirit leads him to confession,
      willingly to confess his sins, nakedly and honestly,
      with great sorrow and great shame that he has so befouled the
        fair image of God.
Then he undertakes penance for every sin, imposed by his confessor
    (which is instructed in Holy Church by the teaching of the
    Holy Spirit).
  And this is one humiliation that much pleases God;
  and also humbly bearing bodily sickness sent from God;
  and also sorrow and shame from without,
  and reproof and despising from the world
  with all kinds of grievance and temptations which we are thrown
    into, bodily and spiritually.

Most preciously our good Lord protects us when it seems to us that
we are nearly forsaken and cast away because of our sin and because
we see that we have deserved it.

And because of the humility that we gain in these troubles, we are
raised very high in God's sight, by His grace.

Also our Lord visits whom He will with particular grace with so
great contrition (also with compassion and true yearning for God)
that they are suddenly released from sin and pain and taken up to
bliss and made equal with the exalted saints.

  By contrition we are made pure,
  by compassion we are made ready,
  and by true yearning for God we are made worthy.

These are three means, as I understand, by which all souls come to
heaven—that is to say, those who have been sinners on earth and
shall be saved.

By these remedies it would be fitting for every soul to be healed.

And even though the soul is healed, its wounds are seen before God,
  not as wounds, but as awards.
 And so contrariwise,
    as we are punished here with sorrow and with penance,
    we shall be rewarded in heaven by the gracious love of our
      Lord God Almighty who wills that no one who comes
      there lose his efforts in any degree,
        for He considers sin as sorrow and pain for His lovers to
          whom because of love He allots no blame.

The recompense that we shall receive shall not be little, but it shall
  be exalted, glorious, and full of honor.

And in this way shall all shame be transformed to honor and more
  joy.

Our gracious Lord does not wish His servants to despair because of
  frequent or grievous falling,
  because our falling does not prevent Him from loving us.

Peace and love are always in us, existing and working, but we are
not always in peace and in love.

However, He wills that we take heed in this way—
  that He is the ground of all our whole life in love, and,
  furthermore, that He is our everlasting protector
    and mightily defends us against all our enemies
    who are most terrible and fierce against us
      (and our need is so much the more because we give those
      enemies opportunity by our falling).

40

It is a supreme friendship of our gracious Lord
    that He protects us so tenderly while we are in our sin.
Furthermore, He touches us most secretly
    and shows us our sin by the sweet light of mercy and grace.
  But when we see ourselves so foul,
  then we imagine that God is angry with us for our sin,
  and then by the Holy Spirit we are guided by contrition to prayer
    and to the desire to amend our life with all our might,
  in order to abate the anger of God,
    until the time that we discover a rest in soul and a quietness in
    conscience.
  Then we hope that God has forgiven us our sins—and it is true.

And then our gracious Lord shows Himself to the soul, all merrily
    and with glad countenance, with friendly greeting, as if the soul
    had been in pain and in prison, saying sweetly thus:
      "My dearly beloved, I am glad thou hast come to me.
      In all thy woe, I have always been with thee,
      and now thou seest my loving and we are one-ed in bliss."

In this way are sins forgiven by mercy and grace
    and our soul honorably received in joy
      (just as it shall be when it comes to heaven)
  as often as it comes
    by the gracious working of the Holy Spirit
    and the virtue of Christ's Passion.

Here I understand truly that everything is prepared for us by the
great goodness of God to such an extent that whenever we are
ourselves in peace and love, we are truly safe.

But because we cannot have this in fullness while we are here,

therefore it is right for us evermore to believe in sweet prayer
and in love-filled yearning with our Lord Jesus. He yearns
ever to bring us to the fullness of joy (as it was said
before where He shows the spiritual thirst).

But now, because of all this spiritual comfort that is spoken of above,
if any man or woman is led by folly
to say or to think: "If this is true, then it would be good to sin in
order to have more reward,"
or else to place less weight on sin,
beware of this leading, for truly, if it comes, it is untrue and from
the enemy.

Because the same true love that touches us all by His blessed
comfort, that same blessed love teaches us that we should
hate sin for the sake of love alone.

And I am certain, from my own experience, that the more every
natural soul sees this in the gracious love of our Lord God,
the more loath it will be to sin,
and the more it will be ashamed.

For if before us were laid all the pains in hell and in purgatory and
on earth, death and all the rest, over against sin,
we ought rather to choose all that pain than sin,
because sin is so vile and so much to be hated,
that it cannot be compared to any pain—if that pain is not sin.

To me was shown no more cruel hell than sin,
for a natural soul has no pain except sin,
and all is good except sin,
and nothing is evil except sin.

And when we direct our attention to love and humility, by the working
of mercy and grace, we are made all fair and pure.

As powerful and as wise as God is to save man,
also He is just as willing to do so.

Christ Himself is the ground of all the customs of Christian men, and
He taught us to do good against evil.

Here we can see that He is Himself this love,
and He does to us as He teaches us to do,
for He wills that we be like Him in wholeness of endless love
for ourselves and
for our fellow Christians.

No more than His love for us is broken off because of our sin,
so no more does He will that our love for ourselves and for our fellow
Christians be broken off.

But unashamedly hate sin and endlessly love the soul as God loves it.
Then would we hate sin just as God hates it,
and love the soul just as God loves it,
for this word that God said is an endless comfort:
"I keep thee full safely."

41

After this our Lord showed regarding prayer
and in this showing I see two applications of our Lord's meaning:
one is rightful prayer,
the other is sure trust.

And yet frequently our trust is not complete,
for we are not certain that God hears us,
because of our unworthiness (as it seems to us)
and because we feel absolutely nothing
(for we are frequently as barren and dry after our prayers as
we were before).

And thus, it is in our feeling, our foolishness, that the cause of our
    weakness lies (for this have I experienced in myself).

And all this brought our Lord suddenly to my mind and He showed
these words and said:
    "I am the ground of thy praying—
        first, it is my will that thou have something,
        and next I make thee to want it,
        and afterwards I cause thee to pray for it.
            If thou prayest for it,
                how, then, could it be that thou wouldst not get what thou
                    askest for?"

And thus in the first proposition, with the three that follow, our good
Lord shows a powerful encouragement, as can be seen
in the above words.

In that first statement, where He says: "if thou prayest for it, etc.,"
    there He shows the very great pleasure and endless reward that
    He will give us because of our praying.

In the second statement, where He says: "How then, could it be?
    etc.,"
    this was said as an impossible thing,
    Because it is the most impossible thing that can be that we
        should pray for mercy and grace and not get it.
    Because everything that our good Lord causes us to pray for,
    He himself has already appointed to us from without beginning.

Here can we see, then,
    that it is not our praying that is the cause of the goodness and
        grace that He does for us,
    but God's own characteristic goodness.

And that He showed truthfully in all those sweet words when He
says, "I am ground. . . ."

And our good Lord wills that this be recognized by His lovers on
    earth

and the more that we recognize this,
the more we shall pray (if it is wisely accepted)
and this is our Lord's intention.

Praying is
    a true, gracious, lasting intention of the soul
    one-ed and made fast to the will of our Lord
    by the sweet, secret working of the Holy Spirit.

Our Lord Himself,
    He is the first receiver of our prayer, as I see it,
    and He accepts it most favorably,
    and, highly rejoicing,
    He sends the prayer up above
    and places it in a Treasury where it shall never perish.

It is there before God with all His holy saints,
    constantly acceptable,
    always assisting our needs;
        and when we shall receive our bliss,
        our prayer shall be given to us as an award of joy
        with endless honor-filled favor from Him.

Most glad and happy is our Lord about our prayer,
    and He watches for it
    and He wishes to enjoy it,
    because with His grace
        it makes us like Himself in character as we are in nature.

And this is His blessed will, for He says this:
    "Pray inwardly even though it seems to give thee no pleasure, for
        it is beneficial enough though thou perceivest it not.

Pray inwardly,
   though thou sensest nothing,
   though thou seest nothing, yea,
   though thou thinkest thou canst achieve nothing,
      for in dryness and barrenness,
      in sickness and in feebleness,
      then is thy prayer completely pleasing to me,
   though it seems to give thee but little pleasure.

And thus all thy living is prayer in my eyes."

Because of the reward and the endless favor that He wishes to give
us for it, He desires to have us pray constantly in His sight.
   God accepts the good intention and the toil of His servants, no
   matter how we feel,
wherefore it pleases Him that we work both in our prayer and in
   good living by His help and His grace,

      reasonably with good sense,
      keeping our strength for Him
      until we have Him whom we seek in fullness of joy,
      that is, Jesus.

         (He showed this word before in the fifteenth revelation:
         "Thou shalt have Me for thy reward.")

And thanksgiving is also part of prayer.
Thanksgiving is
   a true, inner awareness,
   with great reverence and loving awe
   turning ourselves with all our might towards the actions our good
      Lord guides us to,
   rejoicing and thanking Him inwardly.

And sometimes, because of its abundance, thanksgiving breaks out
   with voice and says:

"Good Lord, thanks be to Thee; blessed mayest Thou be!"
And sometimes when the heart is dry and feels nothing
    (or else by temptation of our Enemy)
    then the heart is driven by reason and by grace
    to call upon our Lord with voice,
        recounting His blessed Passion and His great goodness.

And the strength of our Lord's word
    is directed into the soul,
    and enlivens the heart,
    and introduces it by His grace into true practices,
    and causes it to pray most blessedly,
    and truly to delight in our Lord.

That is a most blessed, loving thanksgiving in His sight.

42

Our Lord God wishes for us to have true understanding,
    and especially in three matters which are related to our prayer.

    The first is by whom and how our prayer originates;
        "by whom" He shows when He says, "I am ground . . ."; and
        "how" is by His goodness, for He says, "First, it is my will . . ."
    For the second, in what manner and how we should practice our
        prayers; and that is that our will be transformed into the will
        of our Lord, rejoicing; and this He means when He says, "I
        make thee to will it . . ."
    For the third, that we understand the fruit and the end of our
        prayer: that is, to be one-ed to and like our Lord in everything.

And for this meaning and for this end was all this loving lesson
    shown;
    and He wishes to help us,

if we will make our prayer just as He says Himself—
blessed may He be!

This is our Lord's will:
   that our prayer
   and our trust
      be both equally great.

For if we do not trust as much as we pray,
   we do incomplete honor to our Lord in our prayer,
   and also we delay and pain ourselves;
   and the reason is, as I believe, because
      we do not truly acknowledge that our Lord is the ground on
         which our prayer grows,
   and also that we do not recognize that prayer is given us by the
      grace of His love.
      For if we knew this, it would make us trust that we would
      receive, by our Lord's gift, all that we desire.

For I am certain that no man asks mercy and grace with a true
intention,
   unless that mercy and that grace have been first given to him.

But sometime it comes to our mind
   that we have prayed a long time,
   and yet, we believe that we have not received our request.

However because of this we should not be sad,
for I am certain, in keeping with our Lord's purpose, that either
      we are to await
      a better time,
      or more grace,
      or a better gift.

He wills we have true knowledge that in Himself He is Existence

94

itself; and in this knowledge He wills that our understanding be
grounded with all our might and all our purpose
and all our intention.
And on this foundation He wills that we take our place
and make our dwelling.

By the gracious light of Himself, He wills that we have understanding
of three things that follow:
The first is our noble and excellent creation;
the second, our precious and dearworthy redemption;
the third, everything that He has made beneath us to serve us and
which, for love of us, He protects.

What He means is thus, as if He said:
"Behold and see that I have done all this *before* thy prayer,
and now thou art and thou prayest to Me."
Thus He intends that it is right for us to know that the greatest deeds
are done as Holy Church teaches.

And in contemplating this we ought to pray with gratitude for the
deed that is now being done—
and that is to pray
that He rule us and guide us to His honor in this life,
and bring us to His bliss—
and for that He has done everything.

What He intends is this:
that we understand that He does everything,
and that we pray for that.

For the one is not enough,
for if we pray and do not understand that He does it, it makes
us sad and doubtful, and that is not His honor,
and if we understand what He does, and we do not pray, we

do not our duty. And that way it cannot be, that is to say,
that is not the way He sees it,
but rather to understand that He does it *and* to pray also,
in that way is He honored
and we are helped.

Everything that our Lord has already appointed to do, it is His will
that we pray for that, either in particular or in general.

And the joy and the bliss that that is to Him,
and the favor and honor that we shall have from that,
it surpasses the understanding of all creatures in this life,
as I see it.

Prayer is
a right understanding of that fullness of joy that is to come,
with true yearning and certain trust.
In prayer,
the tasting of our bliss (that we are naturally appointed to)
naturally makes us to yearn;
true understanding and love (with sweet remembrance of our
Savior) graciously makes us trust.
And thus by nature do we yearn,
and by grace do we trust.
And in these two actions, our Lord watches us constantly,
for it is our duty,
and His goodness can assign no less to us.

Therefore, it is proper for us to give our best effort thereto;
and when we have done it,
then shall we still think that it is nothing—
and truly it is nothing.

But we do what we can,
and humbly ask mercy and grace,
and all that we fall short, we shall find in Him.

Thus He means where He says: "I am ground of thy praying."

And thus in this blessed word, along with the showing, I saw a complete victory against all our weakness and all our doubtful fears.

43

Prayer ones the soul to God;
    for though the soul is ever like God in nature and essence
        (restored by grace),
    it is often unlike God in its external state by sin on man's part.

Then is prayer a witness that the soul wills as God wills,
and it comforts the conscience and inclines man to grace.

In this way He teaches us to pray and
mightily to trust that we shall have what we pray for;
    for He looks upon us in love
    and wishes to make us partners in His good will and deed,
    and therefore He moves us to pray for that which it delights Him
        to do.

For these prayers and good will (which we have as His gift), He will
    reward us and give us endless recompense.
    (And this was shown in this word: "If thou prayest for it . . .")

    In this word, God showed as great pleasure and as great delight
    as if He were much beholden to us for every good deed that we do
        (and yet it is He who does it)
    and for the fact we pray to Him mightily to do everything that
        pleases Him, as if He said:
    "How couldst thou please me more than to pray to me mightily,
    wisely, and willingly to do the thing that I am going to do?"

And thus the soul by prayer comes to agree with God.

When our gracious Lord by His particular grace shows Himself to
our soul, we have what we desire,
and then we do not see for that time what more we should pray
for, but all our purpose with all our might is fixed wholly upon
the contemplation of Him.

This is an exalted incomprehensible prayer, as I see it, for the whole
cause for which we pray, is to be one-ed to the vision and the
contemplation of Him to whom we pray,
marvelously rejoicing with reverent fear
and such great sweetness and delight in Him
that for the time being we can pray absolutely nothing
except as He moves us.

I am well aware that the more the soul sees of God,
the more it desires Him by His grace.
But when we do *not* see Him in this way,
then we sense a need and cause to pray—
because of our falling short,
because of the unfitness of ourselves for Jesus.

For when the soul is tempted, troubled, and left to itself by its unrest,
then it is time to pray to make that soul pliant and obedient to
God.
(But by no kind of prayer does one make God pliant to himself, for
He is always the same in love.)

Thus I saw that whenever we see needs for which we pray,
then our good Lord follows us,
helping our desire.

And when we by His special grace plainly gaze upon Him,
seeing no other,
then we need to follow Him
and He draws us into Him by love.
For I saw and sensed that His marvelous and fulsome goodness
completes all our abilities.

Then I saw that His constant working in all manner of things
 is done so well,
 so wisely,
 and so powerfully
that it surpasses all our imagining,
and all that we can suppose and comprehend.

 And then we can do nothing more than to gaze at Him
 and rejoice with a high mighty desire to be wholly
 one-ed to Him,
 and to pay attention to His prompting,
 and rejoice in His loving,
 and delight in His goodness.

Then shall we, with His sweet grace, in our own humble constant
 prayer, come unto Him now in this life by many secret touchings
 of sweet spiritual sights and experiences, meted out to us as our
 simplicity can bear it.

And this is wrought, and shall be, by the grace of the Holy Spirit,
 until we shall die in yearning for love.

And then shall we all come unto the Lord,
 knowing ourselves clearly,
 and possessing God fully,
 and we being eternally completely hidden in God,

 seeing Him truly,
 touching Him fully,
 hearing Him spiritually,
 and delectably smelling Him,
 and sweetly tasting Him.

Then we shall see God face to face, simply and most fully—
 the creature that is created shall see and eternally contemplate
 God who is the Creator.

(For no man can see God in this way and live afterwards—that is to say, in this mortal life—

however, when He of His particular grace wishes to show Himself here, He strengthens the creature beyond itself, and He moderates the showing according to His own will, so that it does good at the time.)

44

God showed frequently in all the revelations that man continually performs His will and His honor everlastingly,

without any ceasing.

(And what this action is was shown in the first revelation, and that on a wonderful basis: for it was shown in the operation of the soul of Our Blessed Lady Saint Mary, by truth and wisdom.)

But I hope, however, by the grace of the Holy Spirit, that I shall say what I saw.

Truth perceives God,
and wisdom contemplates God,
    and from these two comes the third,
and that is a holy, wonderful delight in God, which is love.

Where truth and wisdom are, in truth there is love,
truly coming from them both,
and all are of God's creation.

For He is eternal supreme Truth,
    eternal supreme Wisdom,
        eternal supreme Love uncreated;
    and man's soul is a created thing in God,
    which has the same divine qualities except created.

And continually the soul does what it was made for:

it perceives God,
it contemplates God,
and it loves God.

Because of this God rejoices in the creature and the creature in God,
endlessly marveling.
In this marveling the creature sees his God, his Lord, his Creator,
so high, so great, and so good in reference to himself who is
created, that scarcely does the creature seem anything at all by
himself;
but the clarity and the purity of truth and wisdom cause him to
see and to recognize that he is created because of love and in this
love God endlessly keeps him.

45

God judges us based on the essence of our human nature
which is always kept constantly in Him,
whole and safe without end;
and this judgement comes from His rightfulness.
But man judges based on our changeable fleshliness
which seems now one thing, now another,
according to what it picks from among the parts
and expresses publicly.
And this human judgement is muddled,
for sometimes it is good and gentle,
and sometimes it is cruel and oppressive.
Insofar as it is good and gentle, it is part of rightfulness;
and insofar as it is cruel and oppressive, our good Lord Jesus
reforms it by mercy and grace through the virtue of His
Blessed Passion and so brings it into rightfulness.

And though these two are thus reconciled and one-ed,
still both shall be acknowledged in heaven without end.

The first judgement is of God's rightfulness, and that is from His high
     endless love.
   This is that fair, sweet judgement that was shown in the whole fair
   revelation in which I saw Him assign to us no kind of blame.
     And although this was sweet and delightful,
          yet in the observing of this alone
               I was unable to be fully comforted, because of the judgement
                    of Holy Church which I had understood before and was
                    constantly in my sight.

   And therefore by this Church judgement it seemed to me that it
          was necessary for me to acknowledge myself as a sinner.
   And by the same judgement,
          I acknowledged that sinners are sometimes deserving of blame
               and anger,
          but these two things—blame and anger—I could not find in God.

Therefore my deliberation and desire was more than I know
          or can tell,
     because God Himself showed the higher judgement at the same
          time, and therefore it was necessary for me to accept that—
     but the lower judgement was taught me previously in Holy Church,
          and therefore I could in no way give up that lower judgement.

Then this was my desire:
     that I could see in God
     in what way the judgement of Holy Church here on earth is true
     in His sight,
     and how it is proper for me truly to understand it.
          (By this both judgements could be saved, in so far as it would be
          honorable to God and the morally right way for me.)

To all this I had no other response except an amazing example of a
lord and of a servant (as I shall tell later)—and that most mystically
shown.

And yet I remained in my desire
    (and I will until my end)
    that I could by grace distinguish these two judgements as is proper
    for me—

for all heavenly and all earthly things that belong to heaven,
    are contained in these two judgements,
    and the more knowledge and understanding
    that we have of these two judgements
    by the gracious guiding of the Holy Spirit,
    the more we shall see and understand our failures, and ever the
        more that we see our failings, the more naturally by grace we
        shall yearn to be filled full of endless joy and bliss,
    for we are created for that,
    and the essence of our human nature
    is now blissful in God,
    and has been since it was made,
    and shall be, without end.

46

But the passing life that we have here in our fleshliness does not know what our self is, except in our Faith.

And when we know and see truly and clearly what our self is, then shall we truly and clearly see and know our Lord God in fullness of joy.

And therefore, it is inevitable
    that the nearer we are to our bliss,
    the more we shall yearn—
        and that both by nature and by grace.

We can have knowledge of our self in this life by the continual help
    and strength of our own noble human nature.
In this knowledge, we can increase and grow by the furthering and
    aiding of mercy and grace,

but we can never fully know our self,
until the last point,
　　and at that point this passing life
　　　and all manner of pain and woe shall have an end.

And therefore, it belongs properly to us, both by nature and grace,
to yearn and desire with all our might to know our self
and in this full knowledge we shall truly and clearly know our God
　　in fullness of endless joy.

And yet, during all this time from the beginning to the end of the
　revelation, I had two kinds of observations:
the one was of endless continuing love, with a security of
　　protection and blissful salvation (for the whole showing
　　was about this);
the other was the common teaching of Holy Church, in which
　　teaching I was previously formed and grounded, and was
　　willingly keeping it in practice and in understanding.

And the beholding of all this came not from me,
because I was not by the showing moved nor led from that Church
teaching in any kind of point,
　but in the showing I was rather taught to love that teaching,
　　to delight in it, for by it I could (with the help of our Lord and
　　　His grace)
　grow and rise to more heavenly knowledge and nobler loving.

And thus, in all this beholding it seemed to me to be necessary to see
　and to know that we are sinners,
　and we do many evils that we ought to stop,
　and we leave many good deeds undone that we ought to do.
And for this we deserve pain and blame and wrath.

But notwithstanding all this, I saw truthfully that our Lord was never
　angry, nor ever shall be,
　　for He is God:

He is good,
He is life,
He is truth,
He is love,
He is peace;
and His Power, His Wisdom, His Love, and His Unity do not
allow Him to be angry.
(For I saw truly that it is against the character of His Power
to be angry,
and against the character of His Wisdom,
and against the character of His Goodness.)

God is the goodness that cannot be angry, for He is nothing but
goodness.
Our soul is one-ed to Him, who is unchangeable goodness,
and between God and our soul is neither anger nor forgiveness, as
He sees it.
For our soul is so completely one-ed to God by His own goodness,
that there can be absolutely nothing at all separating God and soul.

To this understanding the soul was led by love and drawn by power
in every showing. That it is thus—and how it is thus—our good Lord
showed truly by His great goodness, and also that He wills that we
desire to comprehend it (that is to say, in so far as it is proper for
His creature to comprehend it).
Everything that this simple soul understood, God wills that it be
shown and know,
for those things which He wishes to keep secret, He Himself
mightily and wisely hides out of love
(for I saw in the same showing that much that is secret is hidden
which can never be known until the time that God of His
goodness has made us worthy to see it).
With this I am well satisfied,
awaiting our Lord's will in this high wonder.

And now I yield myself to my mother, Holy Church,
as a simple child ought.

47

Two objectives belong to our soul by obligation:
  one is that we reverently marvel,
  the other is that we meekly suffer, ever rejoicing in God.

For He wants us to know that we shall in a short time see clearly
within Himself all that we desire.

Notwithstanding all this, I beheld and marveled greatly at the mercy
and forgiveness of God,
  for by the teaching that I had beforehand, I understood that the
  mercy of God was supposed to be the remission of His wrath after
  the time that we have sinned.

  (It seemed to me that to a soul whose intention and desire is to
  love, the wrath of God would be more severe than any other
  pain, and therefore I accepted that the remission of His wrath
  would be one of the principal objectives of His mercy.)

But in spite of anything that I might behold and desire, I could not
see this point in the entire showing.

But how I saw and understood concerning the works of mercy, I shall
say somewhat, in so far as God wishes to give me grace.
  I understood thus:
    man is changeable in this life,
    and by frailty
    and by simplicity
    and lack of cunning,
      being overcome, he falls into sin.

He is impotent and unwise by himself,
    and also his will is overwhelmed during this time he is in
    temptation and in sorrow and woe.

And the cause is blindness, for he sees not God—
    because if he saw God constantly,
    he would have no harmful experience,
    nor disturbance of any kind,
    nor the distress that is a servant to sin.

This I saw and felt at the same time,
    and it seemed to me that the sight and the feeling was noble and
        plenteous and gracious in comparison to what our ordinary
        experience is in this life,
    but yet I thought it was only small and lowly in comparison to the
        great desire that the soul has to see God.

I perceived in me five kinds of operations which are these:
    rejoicing,
    mourning,
    desire,
    fear,
    and certain hope:
        "rejoicing" because God gave me understanding and knowledge
            that it was Himself that I saw;
        "mourning," and that was because of failing;
        "desire," and that was that I might see Him ever more and
            more, understanding and acknowledging that we shall
            never have full rest till we see Him truly and clearly in
            heaven;
        "fear" was because it seemed to me in all that time that that
            vision would fail and I would be left to myself;
        "certain hope" was in the endless love, that I saw I would be
            protected by His mercy and brought to His bliss, and
            rejoicing in His sight with this certain hope of His merciful

107

protection gave me understanding and comfort so that mourning and fear were not greatly painful.

And yet in all this I beheld in the showings of God that this kind of vision of Him cannot be constant in this life—and that for His own honor and for increase of our endless joy.

And therefore we are frequently without the sight of Him,
    and at once we fall into ourselves,
    and then we discover no sense of rightness—nothing but the
        contrariness that is within ourselves
    (and that from the ancient root of our First Sin with all that
    follows after from our own contrivance)
    and in this we are troubled and tempted with a sense of sins and
        of pains in many different ways, spiritually and bodily, as it is
        familiar to us in this life.

48

But our good Lord, the Holy Spirit
    (who is endless life dwelling in our soul)
    full safely keeps us,
    and makes a peace in the soul,
    and brings it to rest by grace,
    and makes it submissive,
    and reconciles it to God.
And this is the mercy and the way in which our Lord constantly leads us as long as we are here in this changeable life.

I saw no wrath except on man's part, and that He forgives in us.
    For wrath is nothing else but a departure from and an opposition
    to peace and to love,
        and either it comes from the failure of power
        or from the failure of wisdom,

or from the failure of goodness
  (which failure is not in God but it is on our part—for we,
  because of sin and miserableness, have in us a wrath and a
  continuing opposition to peace and to love—and that He
  showed very often in His loving demeanor
  of compassion and pity).

The basis of mercy is love,
and the action of mercy is our protection in love;
  and this was shown in such manner
  that I could not conceive of the property of mercy
  in any other way than as if it were all love in love.

That is to say,
  mercy is a sweet, gracious working in love mingled with plenteous
    pity, as I see it.

Mercy works, protecting us,
  and mercy works transforming everything into good for us.

Mercy, out of love, allows us to fail to a limited extent,
and in so far as we fail, in so much we fall;
and in so far as we fall, so much we die;
  for it is necessary that we die
  in as much as we fall short of the sight and sense of God,
  who is our life.

  Our failing is frightful,
  our falling is shameful,
  and our dying is sorrowful;
    but still in all this, the sweet eye of pity and of love never
      departs from us,
    and the working of mercy ceases not.

For I observed the attribute of mercy and I observed the attribute of
grace, which are two kinds of action in one love;

mercy is a pity-filled attribute which belongs to Motherhood in
    tender love,
and grace is a dignified attribute which belongs to royal Lordship
    in the same love.

Mercy works:
    protecting,
    enduring,
    bringing life, and healing,
    and all is from the tenderness of love;
and grace works:
    building up,
    rewarding, and
    endlessly going beyond what our loving and our labor deserves,
    spreading out widely
    and showing the noble, plenteous largesse of God's royal
        Lordship in His marvelous courtesy.

And this is from the abundance of love,
    for grace converts our frightful failing into plenteous endless
        solace,
    and grace converts our shameful falling into noble, honorable
        rising,
    and grace converts our sorrowful dying into holy, blissful life.

I saw full certainly that
    ever as our contrariness makes pain, shame, and sorrow for us
        here on earth,
    just so on the contrary, grace makes solace, honor, and bliss for us
        in heaven,
    exceeding the earthly to such an extent
        that when we come up and receive the sweet reward which
            grace has created for us,
    then we shall thank and bless our Lord, endlessly rejoicing that
        ever we suffered woe.

110

And that shall be because of an attribute of blessed love that we shall discover in God—which we might never have known without woe going before.

And when I saw all this, it was necessary to agree that the mercy of God and the forgiveness is in order to abate and consume *our* wrath, not His.

49

To the soul this was a mighty wonder
    (which was continually shown in all showings,
    and with great diligence observed)
    that our Lord God, as far as He is concerned, cannot forgive—
      because He cannot be angry—it would be impossible.

For this was shown:
    that our life is all based and rooted in love,
    and without love we cannot live.

And therefore to the soul
    (which by His special grace sees so obviously the exalted marvelous goodness of God, and that we are endlessly one-ed to Him in love)

it is the most impossible thing that can be that God would be angry,
    for wrath and friendship are two opposites.

He who lays waste and destroys our wrath and makes us humble and gentle, it is essential for us to believe that He is always clothed in that same love, humble and gentle—which is opposite to wrath.

111

I saw full certainly that where our Lord appears,
peace comes to pass
and wrath has no place.

I saw no kind of wrath in God,
neither for a short time
nor for long.

(For truly, as I see it, if God were to be angry even a hint,
we would never have life nor place nor being.)

As truly as we have our being from the endless Power of God
and from the endless Wisdom
and from the endless Goodness,
just as truly we have our protection in the endless Power of God,
in the endless Wisdom
and in the endless Goodness.

Although we feel miseries,
disputes
and strifes in ourselves,
yet are we all mercifully enwrapped
in the mildness of God and in His humility,
in His kindliness and in His gentleness.

I saw full certainly that all our endless friendship,
our place,
our life, and
our being is in God,
because that same endless goodness that keeps us that we perish
not when we sin,
that same endless goodness continually negotiates in us a peace
against our wrath and our contrary falling,
and with a true fear makes us see our need strongly to seek
unto God in order to have forgiveness with a grace-filled
desire for our salvation.

We may not be blissfully saved until we are truly in peace and in love, for that is our salvation.

Although we
    (by the wrath and the contrariness that is in us)
  are now in tribulation, uneasiness, and woe
    (as it falls to our blindness and frailty)
  yet are we sure and safe by the merciful protection of God
    so that we perish not.

But we are not blissfully safe in possessing our endless joy until we
    are wholly in peace and in love—that is to say,
  fully gratified with God
  and with all His works
  and with all His judgements,
  and loving and peaceable with ourselves
  and with our fellow Christians
  and with all that God loves, as love pleases.
And this God's goodness carries out in us.

    Thus I saw that God is our true peace
  and He is our sure keeper when we are ourselves unpeaceful,
  and He continually works to bring us into endless peace.

And thus, when we, by the action of mercy and grace, are made humble and gentle, we are completely safe. When it is truly at peace in itself, suddenly the soul is one-ed to God,
because in Him is found no wrath.

Thus I saw that when we are wholly in peace and in love, we find no contrariness nor any kind of hindrance.
  And that contrariness which is now in us,
  our Lord God of His goodness makes most profitable for us,
  because that contrariness is the cause of our tribulations and all
    our woe,

and our Lord Jesus takes those
and sends them up to heaven,
and there are they made more sweet and delectable than heart
    can think or tongue can tell,
and when we come there, we shall find them ready,
    all transformed into truly beautiful and endless honors.

Thus is God our steadfast foundation here,
  and He shall be our complete bliss
  and make us unchangeable as He is, when we are there.

50

In this mortal life mercy and forgiveness is our way which evermore
leads us to grace.
    By the temptation and the sorrow that we fall into on our part,
      we are often dead, according to man's judgement on earth,
      but in the sight of God the soul that shall be saved was never
        dead and never shall be.

And yet here I wondered and marveled with all the diligence of my
soul, meaning thus:
    "Good Lord, I see Thee who art very truth
    and I know truly that we sin grievously all day and are much
      blameworthy;
      and I can neither relinquish the knowledge of this truth,
      nor can I see Thee showing to us any manner of blame.
    How can this be?"
        (For I knew by the common teaching of Holy Church and by
        my own sense that the guilt of our sin continually hangs upon
        us, from the First Man unto the time that we come up into
        heaven.)

Then was this a miracle to me:

that I saw our Lord God showing to us no more blame
than as if we were as pure and as holy as angels are in heaven.

Between these two opposites my reason was greatly troubled by my
blindness,
and could have no rest for fear that His blessed Presence would
pass from my sight and I be left in ignorance of how He looks
on us in our sin.
(For either it was necessary for me to see in God that sin was
all done away,
or else it was necessary for me to see in God how He looks at
it—
whereby I could truly recognize how I ought to look at sin and
the manner of our guilt.)

My yearning went on, continually gazing on Him,
and yet I could have no patience because of great dread and
perplexity, thinking:
"If I take it thus—that we are *not* sinners and not blameworthy—it seems likely I would err and fall short of knowledge
of this truth.
But if it is so that we *are* sinners and blameworthy, good Lord,
how can it then be that I cannot see this verity in Thee,
who art my God, my Creator, in whom I desire to see all
truths?"

[Three points make me brave to ask this:
the first is because it is so lowly a thing
(for if it were a lofty thing, I would be terrified);
the second is that it is so ordinary
(for if it were special and secret, also I would be terrified);
the third is that it is necessary for me to be aware of it, as it seems
to me, if I shall live here
(for the sake of the knowledge of good and evil, by which I can,

115

by reason and grace, the more separate the good from the evil,
and love goodness and hate evil,
   as Holy Church teaches).]

I wept inwardly with all my might,
   searching in God for help, meaning thus:
   "Ah, Lord Jesus, King of bliss, how shall I be comforted?
   Who is it that shall teach me and tell me what I need to know, if I
      cannot at this time see it in Thee?"

51

Then our gracious Lord answered in showing very mysteriously a
   wonderful illustration of a lord who has a servant, and He gave
   insight to my understanding of both of them.
      (This insight was shown twice in the lord,
      and the insight was shown twice in the servant;
      then one part was shown spiritually in bodily form,
      and the other part was shown more spiritually,
         without bodily form.)

For the first was thus: I saw two persons in bodily form, that is to
say, a lord and a servant;
   and with this God gave me spiritual understanding.

The lord sits solemnly in repose and in peace, the servant stands
near, before his lord reverently, ready to do his lord's will. The lord
looks upon his servant most lovingly and sweetly, and humbly he
sends him to a certain place to do his will.

The servant not only goes, but he suddenly leaps up and runs in
great haste because of his love to do his lord's will. And immediately
he falls into a deep pit and receives very great injury. Then he groans
and moans and wails and writhes, but he cannot rise up nor help
himself in any way.

In all this, the greatest misfortune that I saw him in was the lack of reassurance, for he could not turn his face to look back upon his loving lord (who was very near to him and in whom there is complete comfort), but like a man who was feeble and witless for the moment, he was intent on his suffering, and waited in woe.

In this woe he endured seven great pains.

> The first was the painful bruising which he received in his falling, which was very painful to him.
>
> The second was the sluggishness of his body.
>
> The third was the weakness resulting from these two.
>
> The fourth, that he was deluded in his reason and stunned in his mind to such an extent that he had almost forgotten his own love to do his lord's will.
>
> The fifth was that he could not rise up.
>
> The sixth was a most amazing pain to me and that was that he lay alone—I looked all about and watched, and neither far nor near, high nor low, did I see any help for him.
>
> The seventh was that the place in which he lay was a huge, hard, and painful one.

I wondered how this servant could humbly endure there all this woe. And I watched deliberately to see if I could discover any failure in him, or if the lord would allot him any blame, and truly there was none seen—for only his good will and his great desire were the cause of his falling, and he was as willing and as good inwardly as when he stood before his lord ready to do his will.

And in the same way his loving lord constantly watched him most tenderly;

> and now with a twofold attitude:
>
> > one outward, most humbly and gently with great
> > compassion and pity
> > (and this was from the first level of the showing);
> >
> > another inward, more spiritual, and this was shown with a

guiding of my understanding to the lord, and by this guiding,
I saw him greatly rejoice, because of the honorable repose
and nobility that he wills and shall bring his servant to by
his plenteous grace
(and this was from that other level of the showing)
and now my understanding led back to the first part of the
showing, keeping both in mind.

Then says this gracious lord in his meaning: "Behold, behold, my
beloved servant! What harm and distress he has received in my
service for my love, yea, and because of his good will! Is it not
reasonable that I reward him for his fright and his dread, his hurt
and his wounds and all his woe? And not only this, but does it not fall
to me to give a gift that is to him better and more honorable than his
own health would have been? Otherwise it seems to me I would be
doing him no favor."

In this an inward, spiritual showing of the lord's meaning settled
into my soul, in which I saw that it was fitting and necessary—
seeing his great goodness and his own honor—that his dearworthy
servant whom he loved so much would be truly and blessedly
rewarded without end beyond what he would have been if he had
not fallen. Yea, and to such an extent that his falling and all the
woe that he had received from it would be transformed into high
and surpassing honor and endless bliss.

At this point the showing of this illustration vanished, and our good
Lord directed my understanding onwards in vision and in showing the rest of the revelations to the end.

But notwithstanding all this diversion, the wonder of the illustration never went from me; for it seemed to me it was given me as
an answer to my desire, and yet I could not perceive in it a full
interpretation for my comfort at that time.

In the servant (who symbolized Adam, as I shall say) I saw many varied characteristics which could by no means be attributed to individual Adam.

And so at that time I remained much in ignorance, because the full interpretation of this wondrous illustration was not given me at that time. In this mysterious illustration the secrets of the revelation are still much hidden, and nevertheless I saw and understood that every showing is full of secrets, and therefore it behooves me now to tell three aspects by which I am somewhat eased.

The first is the beginning of the teaching which I understood in the showing at that original time;

the second is the inner teaching which I have understood in it since then;

the third, all the whole revelation from the beginning to the end (that is to say, concerning this book) which our Lord God of His goodness frequently brings freely to the sight of my understanding.

And these three are so united, as I understand it, that I do not know how to, nor am I able to divide them.

From this three-in-one I gain teaching by which I ought to believe and trust in our Lord God:

that of the same goodness with which He showed it and for the same purpose,

just so of that same goodness and for that same purpose He will explain it to us when that is His will.

Twenty years after the time of the showing (short three months) I received inner teaching, as I shall say:

"It is right for thee to take heed to all the qualities and conditions that were shown in the illustration even though thou thinkest that they are obscure and uninteresting to your sight."

I assented willingly with great desire, looking inwardly with deliberation at all the points and aspects that were shown at the previous time, to as great an extent as my wit and understanding would serve—beginning with my looking at the lord and at the servant,

and the lord's manner of sitting,
and the place that he sat on,
and the color of his clothing and the kind of style,
and his outward expression,
and his nobility and his goodness within;

at the servant's manner of standing
and the place where and how,
at his manner of clothing, the color and the style,
at his outward behavior
and at his inward goodness and his willingness.

The lord that sat solemnly in repose and in peace,
I interpreted that he is God.
The servant that stood before the lord,
I interpreted that he symbolized Adam
(that is to say, one man was shown at that time, and his falling, to make it thereby to be understood how God looks upon a man and his falling, for in the sight of God all mankind is one man and one man is all mankind).
This man was damaged in his strength, and made completely feeble, and he was stunned in his understanding, for he turned away from the gaze of his lord.
But his will was kept wholly in God's sight—for I saw our Lord commend and approve his will
(however, he himself was prevented and blinded from the knowledge of this will, and this is great sorrow and painful upset to him;
for he neither sees clearly his loving lord [who is most humble and gentle to him] nor sees truly what he himself is in the sight of that loving lord).

120

And well I knew,
> when these two elements—the knowledge of self and the knowl-
> > edge of our Lord—are wisely and truly perceived,
> we shall get rest and peace here in part,
> and the fullness of the bliss of heaven, by His plenteous grace.

(This was a beginning of teaching which I saw at that same time by which I could come to recognize how He looks upon us in our sin. And at that time I saw
> that pain alone blames and punishes,
> but our gracious Lord comforts and succors,
> and He is always of glad disposition to the soul,
> loving and yearning to bring us to bliss.)

The place that our Lord sat on was humble, on the barren and desert earth, alone in wilderness. His clothing was wide and long, and most befitting as becomes a lord. The color of his clothing was blue as azure, most grave and fair. His countenance was merciful, the color of his face was light brown with well-shaped features. His eyes were black, most fair and fitting, showing full of loving pity. And within him was a lofty sanctuary, long and broad, all full of eternal heavenliness. And the loving gaze with which he looked upon his servant constantly (and especially when he fell) it seemed to me could melt our hearts for love, and burst them in two for joy.

This beautiful gazing appeared a fitting mixture which was wondrous to see:
> one part was compassion and pity,
> the other was joy and bliss.
> > (The joy and bliss surpassed as far the compassion and pity as heaven is above earth.)

The pity was earthly and the bliss was heavenly.

> The compassion and the pity of the Father was for the falling of
> > Adam, who is His most beloved creation.

121

The joy and bliss were for the falling of His dearworthy Son, who is equal with the Father.

(The merciful vision of His lovely face filled all earth and descended down with Adam into hell,
and with this constant pity Adam was preserved from endless death.
And this mercy and pity dwell with mankind until the time we come up into heaven.)

But Man is blinded in this life,
and therefore we cannot see our Father God as He is.

And whenever He of His goodness wills to show Himself to Man,
He shows Himself humbly *as* man
(notwithstanding that, I understood truly we ought to know and believe that the Father is *not* man).

And His sitting on the bare earth and desert is to mean this—
He made Man's soul to be His own City and His dwelling place (which is the most pleasing to Him of all His works),
and whenever man had fallen into sorrow and pain he was not wholly fit to serve in that noble position;
and therefore our kind Father rather than give Himself any other
space, sits upon the earth, awaiting mankind
(who are muddled with earth)
until whenever by His grace His dearworthy Son had brought again His City into its noble beauty with His harsh labor.

The blueness of His clothing symbolizes His steadfastness.
The brownness of His fair face with the fitting blackness of the eyes was most agreeable to show His holy gravity.
The breadth of His clothing which was beautiful and flamboyant, symbolizes that He has enclosed within Himself all heavens and all joy and bliss.

(And this was shown in one stroke where I say "my understanding was guided to the Lord." In this guiding I saw Him highly rejoicing because of the honorable restoration that He wills and shall bring His servant to by His plenteous grace.)

And still I wondered, examining the lord and the servant as I said before. I saw the lord sit solemnly and the servant standing reverently before his lord.

In the servant there is a double meaning:
  one outward,
  another inward.

    Outwardly, he was clad humbly as a workman who was used to hard labor, and he stood very near the lord (not right in front of him, but partly aside on the left). His clothing was a white tunic, thin, old and all soiled, stained with sweat of his body, tight fitting for him and short, as it were but a hand's width below the knee, undecorated, seeming as if it would soon be worn out, about to be turned to rags and torn.
    And in this I marveled greatly, thinking: "This is now unfitting clothing for the servant that is so highly loved to stand before so dignified a lord."

    But inwardly, in the servant was shown a foundation of love which he had for the lord which was equal to the love that the lord had for him. The wisdom of the servant saw inwardly that there was one thing to do which would be to the honor of the lord. And the servant, for love, having no regard for himself nor to anything that might befall him, hastily leaped up and ran at the bidding of his lord to do that thing which was the lord's will and his honor.

  For it seemed by his outward clothing that he had been a regular workman for a long time;

and by the insight that I had (both in the lord and in the servant), it
   seemed that he was new, that is to say, newly beginning to
   labor—as a servant who had never been sent out before.

There was a treasure in the earth which the lord loved. I marveled
and imagined what it could be.
   And I was answered in my understanding: "It is a food which is
   lovely and pleasant to the lord."
      (For I saw the lord sit as a man, but I saw neither food nor
      drink wherewith to serve him; that was a wonder.
      Another wonder was that this solemn lord had no servant but
      one, and him he sent out.)

I watched,
   wondering what kind of work it might be
   that the servant would do.

Then I understood that he would do the greatest work and hardest
   toil that is—he would be a gardener;
   digging and ditching,
   straining and sweating,
   and turning over the earth,
   and seeking the depths,
   and watering the plants on time.
      And in this he would continue his labor
      and make sweet streams to run,
      and noble and plenteous fruits to spring, which he would bring
      before the lord and serve him therewith to his delight.

And he would never return until he had prepared this food all ready
as he knew that it delighted the lord, and then he would take this
food with the drink, and bear it most honorably before the lord.

And all this time the lord would sit in the same place awaiting his
servant whom he sent out.

(I still wondered from whence the servant came, for I saw that
the lord had within himself endless life and all kinds of goodness,
except that treasure that was on the earth—and that was grounded
in the lord in wondrous depth of endless love [but it was not wholly
to his honor until this servant had dug it thus nobly and brought it
before him, in himself present]. And except for the lord there was
nothing but wilderness. And I did not understand all that this
illustration meant, and therefore I wondered whence the servant
came.)

In the servant is included the Second Person in the Trinity,
and also in the servant is included Adam, that is to say, all men.
   (And therefore, when I say "the Son," it means the Godhead
   which is equal with the Father, and when I say "the servant," it
   means Christ's manhood which is true Adam.)

By the nearness of the servant is understood the Son, and by the
standing on the left side is understood Adam.

   The lord is the Father, God.
   The servant is the Son, Christ Jesus.
   The Holy Spirit is equal Love who is in Them both.

When Adam fell, God's Son fell—

   because of the true union which was made in heaven,
   God's Son could not be separated from Adam
      (for by "Adam" I understand "all men").

   Adam fell from life to death into the pit of this miserable world
      and after that into hell.
   God's Son fell with Adam into the pit of the womb of the Maiden
      (who was the fairest daughter of Adam) and that in order
      to obtain for Adam exemption from guilt in heaven and on
      earth. And he mightily fetched Adam out of hell.

125

By the wisdom and goodness that was in the servant is understood
   God's Son.
By the poor clothing as a workman standing near the left side is
   understood the manhood of Adam, with all the misfortune and
   weakness that follow from that—
   for in all this our Good Lord showed His own Son and Adam as
      but one man.

The virtue and the goodness that we have is from Jesus Christ, the
weakness and the blindness that we have is from Adam—both of
which were shown in the servant.

And thus has our good Lord Jesus taken upon Himself all our guilt;
and therefore our Father can, and will, no more assign blame to us
than to
His own Son, dearworthy Christ.

In this way He was the servant before His coming onto the earth,
   standing ready before the Father intentionally until whatever
   time the Father would send Him to do that honorable deed by
   which mankind was brought again into heaven—that is to say,
   notwithstanding that He is God (equal with the Father as
   concerns the Godhead) in His foreseeing purpose He was
   willing to be man to save man by fulfilling His Father's will.

So He stood before His Father as a servant, willingly taking upon
   Himself all our burden.
And then He leaped up wholly ready at the Father's will,
and soon He fell most lowly into the Maiden's womb, having no
   regard for Himself nor for His harsh pains.

   The white tunic is His flesh;
      its thinness is that there was absolutely nothing separating the
         Godhead and manhood;
      the tightness of the tunic is poverty;

the age is from Adam's wearing it;
the staining of sweat, from Adam's toil;
the shortness shows the servant's work.

And thus I saw the Son standing, saying in His meaning,
"Behold, my dear Father, I stand before Thee in Adam's tunic all
ready to jump up and to run. I am willing to be on the earth to do
Thine honor when it is Thy will to send me. How long shall I wish
for it?"
(Most truly was the Son aware when it was the Father's will
and how long He would wish for it—that is to say, from the
point of view of His Godhead, for He is the Wisdom of the
Father.)

Therefore this meaning was shown in understanding about the manhood of Christ:
all mankind that shall be saved by the sweet incarnation and
blissful Passion of Christ, all is the manhood of Christ,
for He is the Head
and we are His members
(to which members the day and the time is unknown when
every passing woe and sorrow shall have an end, and the
everlasting joy and bliss shall be fulfilled—which day and
time, all the company of heaven yearns to see).

All who are under heaven who shall come to heaven, their way is by
yearning and desire.
This desire and yearning was shown in the servant standing before
the lord
(or else thus, in the Son's standing before the Father in Adam's
tunic),
for the yearning and desire of all mankind that shall be saved was
manifested in Jesus
(for Jesus is all that shall be saved
and all that shall be saved is Jesus),

127

and all from the love of God, with obedience, meekness and patience,
and virtues that belong to us.

Also in this marvelous illustration I receive a teaching within me
(as it were the beginning of an ABC)
whereby I can have some understanding of our Lord's meaning,
because the secrets of the revelation are hidden in this
illustration (notwithstanding that all the showings are full of
secrets).

The sitting of the Father symbolizes His Godhead
(that is to say, in order to show repose and peace,
for in the Godhead can be no toil).
And that He showed Himself as lord symbolizes our manhood.
The standing of the servant symbolizes labor.
That he stands on the side and on the left symbolizes that he was not
fully worthy to stand directly before the lord.
His leaping up was the Godhead,
and the running was the manhood
(for the Godhead leaps from the Father into the Maiden's womb,
descending into the taking of our human nature; and in this
falling He received great injury; the injury that He received was
our flesh in which He also soon had powerful experiences of
mortal pains).
By the fact that He stood fearfully before the lord, and not directly
so, indicates that His clothing was not respectable enough to
stand directly before the lord, and that could not, or would not,
be His position while He was a workman.
And also He could not sit in repose and peace with the lord until
He had won His peace properly with His harsh toil.
By the left side symbolizes that the Father left His own Son willingly
in the manhood to suffer all man's pains without sparing
Himself.
By the fact that His tunic was at the point of being turned to rags
and torn is understood the stripes and the scourges,

128

the thorns and the nails,
the pulling and the dragging,
His tender flesh tearing
> (as I saw to some degree, the flesh was torn from the skull,
> falling in shreds until the time the bleeding stopped; and then
> the flesh began to dry again, clinging to the bone).

And by the wallowing and writhing, groaning and moaning, is understood that He could never rise omnipotently from the time that He was fallen into the Maiden's womb until His body was slain and dead, He yielding His soul into the Father's hands along with all mankind for whom He was sent.

And at this point of rising He began first to show His power, for He went into hell, and when He was there He raised up out of the deep darkness the Great Root of Jesse which properly was knit to Him in high heaven.
The body was in the grave until Easter morning, and from that time on He lay down never more.
Then was rightfully ended the wallowing and the writhing, the groaning and the moaning; and our foul mortal flesh that God's Son took upon Himself
> (which was Adam's old tunic, tight, bare, and short
then by our Savior was made fair, new, white, and bright, and of endless purity, wide and long, fairer and richer than was then the clothing which I saw on the Father,
> for that clothing was blue,
> and Christ's clothing is now of a light, becoming
> mixture which is so wonderful that I cannot
> describe it, for it is all of true glory).

No longer does the Lord sit on the ground in wilderness, but now He sits on His noblest throne which He made in heaven most to His pleasure.
No longer stands the Son before the Father as a servant fearfully,

plainly clad, in part naked, but now He stands before the Father
directly, richly clad in blessed ampleness, with a crown upon His
Head of precious richness
(for it was shown that we are His crown,
which crown is the Father's joy,
the Son's honor,
the Holy Spirit's pleasure,
and endless marvelous bliss to all that are in heaven).

Now the Son does not stand before the Father on the left side as a
workman, but He sits on His Father's right hand in endless
repose and peace.
(But it is not meant that the Son sits on the right hand, side by
side, as one man sits by another in this life; for there is no such
sitting, as to my sight, in the Trinity for He sits on His Father's
right hand, that is to say, in the highest nobility of the Father's
joys.)

Now is the Spouse, God's Son, in peace with His beloved Wife,
which is Holy Church, the Fair Maiden of endless joy.

Now sits the Son, true God and Man, in repose and peace in His
City, which His Father has devoted to Him out of His endless
purpose,
and the Father is in the Son,
and the Holy Spirit in the Father and in the Son.

52

Thus I saw that
God rejoices that He is our Father,
God rejoices that He is our Mother, and
God rejoices that He is our true Spouse and that our soul is His
beloved wife.

And Christ rejoices that He is our Brother,
and Jesus rejoices that He is our Savior.

These are five high joys, as I understand, in which He wishes that we
rejoice: praising Him, thanking Him, loving Him,
endlessly blessing Him.

All we who shall be saved, for the period of this life, have in us a
wondrous mixture both of well and woe:
    we have in us our Lord Jesus arisen;
    we have in us the misery of the misfortune of Adam's falling.

    Dying, we are steadfastly protected by Christ, and by His gracious
        touching we are raised in certain trust of salvation.
    And by Adam's falling we are so fragmented in our feeling in
        differing ways (by sins and by various pains, in which we are
        made sad and blind as well) that scarcely do we know how to
        obtain any comfort.

    But in our intention we await God and faithfully trust to receive
        mercy and grace;
    and this is His own working in us.

Of His goodness He opens the eye of our understanding by which we
have insight—sometime more and sometime less—as God gives us
ability to receive it.

And now we are raised into one, and again we are allowed to fall
into the other.

And thus is this mixture so wondrous in us that scarcely do we know
about our selves or about our fellow Christians how we hold out,
because of the wonderment of these different feelings—
    except for that same holy assent that we consent to God when we
    sense Him, truly willing to be with Him with all our heart, with all
    our soul, and with all our strength.

131

And then we hate and despise our evil stirrings and all that might be occasion of sin, spiritually and bodily.

And yet nevertheless when this sweetness is hidden, we fall again into blindness, and so into woe and tribulation in diverse ways.

But then this is our comfort:
that we know in our faith that by the strength of Christ, who is our protector, we never consent to sin, but we rail against it, and endure in pain and woe, praying until that time when He shows Himself again to us.

And thus we remain in this muddle all the days of our lives.

But He wills that we trust that He is everlastingly with us, and that in three ways:
He is with us in heaven, true man in His own Person drawing us upward (and that was shown in the spiritual thirst);
and He is with us on earth, leading us (and that was shown in the third showing, where I saw God in a point);
and He is with us in our soul eternally dwelling, ruling and taking care of us (and that was shown in the sixteenth showing, as I shall say).

Thus in the servant was shown the misfortune and blindness of Adam's falling,
and in the servant was also shown the wisdom and goodness of God's Son.

In the lord was shown the compassion and pity for Adam's woe;
and in the lord was also shown the high nobility and the endless honor that mankind has come to by virtue of the Passion and the death of His dearworthy Son.

Therefore He powerfully rejoices in Adam's falling, because of the

132

noble raising and fullness of bliss that mankind has come to, surpassing what we would have had if Adam had not fallen.

And thus in order to see this surpassing nobility my understanding was led to God at the same time that I saw the servant fall.

And so we have now cause for mourning,
    for our sin is the cause of Christ's pains;
and we have everlastingly cause for joy,
    for endless love caused Him to suffer.

Therefore the creature who sees and senses the working of love by grace hates nothing but sin;
    for of all things, as I see it, love and hate are the most unyielding and most immoderate opposites.

Notwithstanding all this, I saw and understood in our Lord's purpose
    that we cannot in this life keep us from sin as totally in complete purity as we shall in heaven.
    But by grace we can well keep ourselves from the sins which would lead us to endless pain (as Holy Church teaches us) and avoid the venial ones, reasonably within our power;
    and, if at any time we fall by our blindness and our misery,
        that we can readily arise,
        knowing the sweet touching of grace, and
        willingly amend ourselves following the teaching of Holy Church according to the sin's gravity,
        and go forthwith to God in love.

Neither on the one hand fall overly low, inclining to despair,
nor on the other hand be over reckless as if we gave no heed,
    but humbly knowing our weakness,
        aware that we cannot stand even a twinkling of an eye except by the protection of grace,
    and reverently cleaving to God,
    trusting in Him alone.

For one way is God's point of view,
and the other way is man's point of view;
  for it belongs to man humbly to accuse himself,
  and it belongs to the excellent goodness of our Lord God graciously
    to forgive man.

These are two parts that were shown in the double attitude in which
the lord viewed the falling of his beloved servant.
  The one was shown outward, very humbly and gently, with great
    compassion and pity,
  and the other of inward endless love.

And just so wills our Lord that we accuse ourselves,
    willingly and truly seeing and recognizing
    our falling and all the harms that come therefrom,
        understanding and being aware that we can never
        reinstate it,
  and along with that that we also willingly and truly recognize and
    acknowledge His everlasting love that He has for us, and His
    plenteous mercy.

Thus graciously to recognize and acknowledge both together is the
gentle self-accusing that our Lord asks of us, and He Himself does it
wherever it happens.

This is the lower part of man's life and it was shown in the outward
expression, in which showing I saw two parts:
  the one is the pitiful falling of man,
  the other is the honorable amends that our Lord has made for
    man.

The other expression was shown inwardly, and that was more exalted
and all the same;
  for the life and the strength that we have in the lower part is from
  the higher, and it comes down to us from the self's natural love by
  grace.

There is absolutely nothing separating the one and the other, for it is all one love.

This blessed love has now in us a double action:
> for in the lower part are
> pains and sufferings,
> compassions and pities,
> mercies and forgiveness
> and such other things that are beneficial,
> but in the higher part are none of these, except the same high love and overwhelming joy, in which overwhelming joy all pains are wholly destroyed.

In this our good Lord showed not only our excusing, but also the honorable nobility that He shall bring us to, transforming all our guilt into endless honor.

53

I saw that He wishes us to be aware that He does not take the falling of any creature that shall be saved more severely than He took the falling of Adam
> (who we know was endlessly loved and safely protected in the time of all his need, and now is blissfully restored in high, surpassing joys)
for our Lord God is so good, so gentle, and so gracious that He can never assign fault to those in whom He shall ever be blessed and praised.

And in this that I have now said my desire was in part answered, and my great fear somewhat eased by the loving, gracious showing of our Good Lord.
> In this showing I saw and understood full certainly that in every soul that shall be saved is a divine will that never consents to sin, nor ever will.

This will is so good that it can never will evil, but evermore continually it wills good and does good in the sight of God.

Therefore our Lord wishes that we recognize this
    in the Faith and the Belief of the Church
    and specifically and truly that we have all this blessed will whole
        and safe in our Lord Jesus Christ,
for that kind of human nature with which heaven shall be filled ought properly, by God's righteousness, to be so knit and one-ed to Him that in that human nature is guarded an essence which can never be (nor should be) parted from Him—and that through His own good will in His endless foreseeing purpose.

Notwithstanding this rightful knitting and this eternal one-ing, still
    the redemption and the buying back of mankind is necessary and
    beneficial in every instance,
since it is done for the same intention and to the same end that Holy Church in our Faith teaches us.

I saw that God never *started* to love mankind,
    for just as mankind shall be in endless bliss fulfilling the joy of God
        as regards His works,
    just so the same mankind has been, in the foresight of God, known
        and loved from without beginning in His rightful intention.

By the endless intention and consent of the full agreement of all the Trinity,
    the Mid-Person wished to be ground and head of this fair human
        nature,
    out of Whom we are all come,
    in Whom we are all enclosed,
    into Whom we shall all go,
    in Him finding our full heaven in everlasting joy
        by the foreseeing purpose of all the blessed Trinity
        from without beginning.

Before ever He made us, He loved us,
and when we were created we loved Him.
   And this is a love created
      by the natural essential Goodness of the Holy Spirit,
      mighty by reason of the Power of the Father,
      and wise in reminder of the Wisdom of the Son,
         and thus is man's soul made by God
         and at the same moment knit to God.

Thus I understand that man's soul is created out of nothing—that is
      to say it is created, but out of nothing that has been created,
      like this:
   when God wished to create man's body,
      He took the slime of earth
         (which is a material mixed and gathered for all physical
            creatures)
      and out of that He created man's body.
   But for the creating of man's soul,
      He willed to take absolutely nothing,
      but He created it.

And thus is the human nature created rightfully one-ed to the
      Creator—
   who is Essential Nature uncreated:
   that is, God.
And therefore it is that there can, and will be, absolutely nothing
separating God and man's soul.

In this endless love man's soul is kept whole
   as the matter of the revelations means and shows;
In this endless love we are led and protected by God
   and never shall be lost,
      for He wishes us to be aware
         that our soul has a life which,
         of His goodness and His grace,

137

shall last in heaven without end,
    loving Him,
    thanking Him,
    praising Him.
And just as we shall exist without end,
so too we were treasured in God,
   and hidden,
     known,
   and loved from without beginning.

Wherefore, He wishes us to be aware
   that the noblest being that ever He made is mankind
     (and the fullest essence
     and the highest virtue
     is the blessed soul of Christ).

Furthermore He wishes us to be aware that mankind's dearworthy
soul was preciously knit to Him in the creation—
   and this knot is delicate and so powerful that it is one-ed into God.
   In this one-ing it is made endlessly holy.

Furthermore, He wishes us to be aware that all the souls that shall
be saved in heaven without end
   are knit and one-ed in this one-ing,
   and made holy in this holiness.

54

Because of the great endless love that God has towards all mankind,
   He makes no distinction in love between
   the blessed soul of Christ
   and the least soul that shall be saved.

It is very easy to believe and to trust that the dwelling of the blessed
soul of Christ is utterly high in the glorious Godhead,

but truly, as I understand in our Lord's meaning,
where the blessed soul of Christ is,
there is the essence of all the souls
that shall be saved within Christ.

We ought highly to rejoice that God dwells in our soul, and much
more highly to rejoice that our soul dwells in God.
Our soul is created to be God's dwelling place, and the dwelling
place of the soul is God, who is uncreated.

It is an exalted understanding inwardly to see and to know
that God who is our Creator dwells in our soul;
and it is a more exalted understanding inwardly to see and to know
that our soul, which is created,
dwells in God's essence—
from which essence, by God,
we are what we are.

I saw no difference between God and our essence,
but just as if it were all God,
and yet my understanding accepted that our essence is in God—that
is to say, that God is God, and our essence is a creation of God.

The all Powerful truth of the Trinity is our Father, for He created us
and keeps us within Him;
and the deep Wisdom of the Trinity is our Mother in whom we are
all enclosed;
the exalted Goodness of the Trinity is our Lord and in Him we are
enclosed and He in us.
We are enclosed in the Father,
we are enclosed in the Son,
and we are enclosed in the Holy Spirit;
and the Father is enclosed in us,
and the Son is enclosed in us,
and the Holy Spirit is enclosed in us:

all Power,
all Wisdom,
all Goodness,
   one God,
   one Lord.

And our faith is a virtue that comes
   from our natural essence
   into our fleshly soul by the Holy Spirit,
and within this virtue all our virtues come to us
   (for without that no man may receive virtue).

Faith is nothing else but a right understanding (with true belief and
     certain trust) of our being—
   that we are in God,
   and God in us—
which we do not see.

And this virtue of faith
   (with all others that God has ordained to us coming within it)
works great things in us,
   for Christ's merciful working is in us
     (and we graciously reconciling to Him through the gifts and the
     virtues of the Holy Spirit),
and this working causes us to be Christ's children
and Christian in living.

55

Thus Christ is our Way,
   safely leading us in His laws,
and Christ in His Body powerfully bears us up to heaven.

I saw that Christ,
   having in Him all of us who shall be saved by Him,
graciously presents his Father in heaven with us.

And this present most thankfully His Father receives and courteously gives it to His Son, Jesus Christ.

This gift and action is joy to the Father
and bliss to the Son
and delight to the Holy Spirit.

And of everything that is proper to us,
it is most delight to our Lord that we rejoice in this joy which is in the blessed Trinity because of our salvation.

(This was seen in the ninth showing
where it speaks more of this matter.)

Notwithstanding all our feeling, woe or well, God wills that we understand and believe that we exist more truly in heaven than on earth.

Our faith comes
from the natural love of our soul
and from the clear light of our reason
and from the steadfast remembrance
which we have of God in our first creation.

At the time that our soul is breathed into our body (at which time we are made fleshly)
also quickly mercy and grace begin to work,
having charge of us and protecting us with pity and love.

In this action the Holy Spirit forms in our faith the hope
that we shall come again up to our essence,
into the strength of Christ,
increased and fulfilled through the Holy Spirit.

Thus I understand that the fleshliness is based in nature,
> in mercy,
> and in grace,

and this basis enables us to receive gifts which lead us to endless life.

For I saw most certainly that our essence is in God, and also I saw that God is in our fleshliness,
> for at the self-same moment that our soul is made fleshly,
> at the same moment is the City of God established in our soul from
> > without beginning.

Into that City He comes and never shall remove it,
> for God is never out of the soul
> in which He dwells blissfully without end.

> > (This was seen in the sixteenth showing where it says: "The place that Jesus takes in our soul, He shall never remove it.")

All the gifts that God can give to creatures He has given to His Son Jesus for us.
> These gifts He, dwelling in us, has enclosed in Himself until the time that we are grown and matured,
> > our soul with our body
> > and our body with our soul
> > > (either of them taking help from the other),

> until we are brought up in stature as nature works, and then, on the basis of human nature
> > with the action of mercy,

> the Holy Spirit graciously breathes into us the gifts leading to
> > endless life.

Thus was my understanding led by God
> > to perceive in Him and to understand,
> > to be aware and to know,
> > that our soul is a "created trinity,"

like to the uncreated blessed Trinity
   (known and loved from without beginning)
and in its creation it is joined to the Creator as it is aforesaid.

This sight was most sweet and wondrous to behold,
   peaceable and restful,
   safe and delightful.

And because of the honorable one-ing that was thus brought about
by God between the soul and body,
   it is inevitable that mankind should be brought back
      from double death.

This bringing back could never be until the time that the Second
      Person in the Trinity had taken the lower part of mankind
   (He to whom the highest part was one-ed in the first creation) and
      these two parts were in Christ
      —the higher and the lower—
   which is but one soul.

   In Christ,
      the higher part was one in peace with God
         in full joy and bliss;
      the lower part, which is fleshly, suffered for
         the salvation of mankind.

      (These two parts were seen and experienced in the eighth
      showing, in which my body was filled with the experience
      and memory of Christ's passion and His death—and fur-
      thermore, with this was an ethereal feeling and secret
      inward vision of the high part that I was shown at that
      same time [when I could not on account of the intermedi-
      ary's suggestion look up into heaven],
      and that was because of the powerful vision of the inner
      life, and this inner life is that exalted essence, that precious
      soul, which is endlessly rejoicing in the Godhead.)

56

Thus I saw most surely
   that it is easier for us to come to the knowledge of God than to
      know our own soul,
      for our soul is so profoundly based in God,
      and so endlessly treasured,
      that we may not come to the knowledge of it
      until we first have knowledge of God,
      who is the Creator to whom it is one-ed.

But, nevertheless, I saw that we have by our human nature a fullness
      of desire wisely and truly to know our own soul,
   and by this desire we are taught to seek our soul where it is,
   and that is in God.

Thus by the gracious leading of the Holy Spirit,
   we must know them both in one,
   whether we are stirred to know God or our soul.
Both stirrings are good and true.

God is nearer to us than our own soul,
   because He is the foundation on which our soul stands
   and He is the means that keeps the essence and the fleshliness
      together so that they shall never separate.

For our soul sits in God in true repose,
and our soul stands in God in true strength,
and our soul is naturally rooted in God in endless love.
   And therefore if we wish to have knowledge of our soul and
   communion and conversation with it, it behooves us that we search
   into our Lord God in whom it is enclosed.

   (And of this enclosing I saw and understood more
   in the sixteenth showing, as I shall say.)

144

And regarding our essence, it can rightly be called our soul, and regarding our fleshliness, it, too, can rightly be called our soul
(and that is because of the one-ing that it has in God).

The honorable City that our Lord Jesus sits in,
   it is our fleshliness in which He is enclosed;
and our natural essence is enclosed in Jesus with the blessed soul of
   Christ sitting in repose in the Godhead.

I saw most surely that is inevitable that we must be in yearning and in penance until the time that we are led so deeply into God that we honestly and truly know our own soul.

And truly I saw that into this great divine depth our good Lord Himself leads us
   in the same love in which He created us,
   and in the same love that He bought us by mercy and grace
      by virtue of his blessed Passion.

Notwithstanding all this,
   we can never come to full knowledge of God
   until we first know clearly our own soul,

   for until the time that the soul is in its full powers,
   we cannot be all fully holy—
      and that is as soon as our fleshliness
      (by the virtue of Christ's Passion)
      is brought up into the essence
         with all the benefits of our tribulation
         that our Lord shall cause us to gain
         by mercy and grace.

I had a partial touching, and it is grounded in nature (that is to say, our reason is based in God who is essential nature).

145

From this essential nature of God mercy and grace spring and
    expand into us,
    accomplishing all things in completing our joy.

These three are our foundations on which we have our being, our
growth, and our fulfillment—
    for in our *human nature* we have our life and our being,
    and in *mercy* and *grace* we have our growth and our fulfillment.

These are three aspects of one goodness,
    and where one works, all work,
    in the things which are now proper to us.

God wills that we understand,
desiring with all our heart and all our strength
to have knowledge of these three more and more
until the time that we are fulfilled.
    For fully to know them
    and clearly to see them
    is nothing else but the endless joy and bliss
    that we shall have in heaven
            (which God wills we begin here in knowledge of His love).

For by our reason alone we cannot benefit,
    unless we have memory and love with it equally;
nor can we be saved only with reference to our natural origin that
    we have in God,
    unless we have, coming from the same origin, mercy and grace.

From these three acting all together we receive all our goods;
    the first of which is the good of human nature
    (for in our first creation God gave to us as many goods and even
greater goods than we could receive in our spiritual essence alone,
but His foreseeing purpose in His endless wisdom willed that we
be two-fold in our human natures).

146

57

Regarding our essence, He made us so noble and so rich that we
constantly work His will and His honor.
   (When I say "we," it means "men who will be saved"; for truly
   I saw that we are what He loves, and we do what He desires
   constantly without any ceasing.)

And from these great riches and from this high nobility, virtues
beyond measure come to our soul when it is knit to our body
   (in which knitting we are made fleshly).

Thus in our essence we are complete,
and in our fleshliness we are insufficient.
   This insufficiency God will restore
   and make complete
   by the action of mercy and grace
   plenteously flowing into us from His own natural goodness.

So His natural goodness causes mercy and grace to work in us, and
the natural goodness that we have from Him enables us to receive
   that working of mercy and grace.

I saw that our human nature is completely within God. In this human
nature
   He makes diversities flowing out of Him to work His will;
   nature protects it,
   and mercy and grace restore and complete it,
   and of these none shall perish.

For our human nature (which is the higher part) is knit to God in
creation; and God is knit to our human nature (which is the lower
part) in the taking of our flesh.

Thus in Christ our two natures are united,
>   for the Trinity is encompassed in Christ in whom our higher part is
>   based and rooted,
>   and our lower part the Second Person has taken, which human
>   nature was first assigned to Him.

I saw most certainly that all the works God has done, or ever shall
do, were completely known to Him and foreseen from without
beginning,
>   and for love He made mankind
>   and for the same love He Himself was willing to be man.

The next good that we receive is our Faith in which our benefiting
>   begins;
>   and it comes from the high riches of our natural essence into our
>   fleshly soul;
>   and it is based in us and we in it
>   >   through the natural goodness of God
>   >   by the working of mercy and grace.

From Faith comes all other goods by which we are guided and saved.

The commandments of God come in our Faith
>   (about which we ought to have two kinds of understanding which
>   are:
>   >   His bidding to love them and to keep them; the other is that we
>   >   ought to know His
>   >   >   forbiddings in order to hate and to refuse them;
>   for in these two are all our actions contained).

Also in our Faith come the Seven Sacraments
>   (each following the other in order as God has ordained them to us)
>   and all manner of virtues
>   >   (for the same virtues that we received from our essence, given to
>   >   us in human nature, by the goodness of God, these same virtues,

148

by the action of mercy, are also given to us in grace, renewed
through the Holy Spirit).

These virtues and gifts are treasured for us within Jesus Christ,
for at that same time that God knitted Him to our body
in the Maiden's womb, He assumed our fleshly soul.
In taking this fleshly soul, He, having enclosed us all in Himself,
one-ed our fleshly soul to our essence.
In this one-ing He was complete humanity, for Christ, having knit
unto Himself all men who shall be saved, is Perfect Man.

Thus Our Lady is our Mother in whom we are all enclosed and out of
her we are born in Christ
(for she who is Mother of our Savior is mother of all who shall be
saved within our Savior).

And our Savior is our true Mother in whom we are endlessly born
and never shall come to birth out of Him.

Plenteously and completely and sweetly was this shown
(and it is spoken of in the first showing where He says that we are
all enclosed in Him and He is enclosed in us; and it is spoken of in
the sixteenth showing where it says that He sits in our soul).

It is His delight to reign in our understanding blissfully,
and to sit in our soul restfully,
and to dwell in our soul endlessly,
drawing us all into Him.

In this drawing He wishes that we be His helpers,
giving Him all our attention,
learning His lesson,
keeping His laws,
desiring that all be done which He does,
honestly trusting in Him—
for truly I saw that our essence is in God.

149

58

God, the blessed Trinity (who is everlasting Existence)
   just as He is endless from without beginning,
   just so it was in His endless purpose to create mankind.

This fair human nature was first assigned to His own Son, the Second Person.
   And when He wished, by full accord of all the Trinity,
   He created us all at once,
   and in our creation He knit us and one-ed us to Himself.

By this one-ing we are kept as pure and as noble as we were created.
By the virtue of the same precious one-ing,
   we love our Maker
   and delight Him,
     praising Him,
     and thanking Him,
     and endlessly rejoicing in Him.
And this one-ing is the action which is done constantly in every soul
     that shall be saved
   (which is the divine will in the soul mentioned before).

Thus in our creation,
   God All Power is our natural Father,
   and God All Wisdom is our natural Mother,
   with the Love and the Goodness of the Holy Spirit—
     who is all one God, one Lord.
And in the knitting and in the one-ing,
   He is our most true Spouse,
   and we are His beloved Wife and His fair Maiden.
     With this Wife He is never displeased, for He says:
     "I love thee and thou lovest me,
     and our love shall never be separated in two."

I beheld the action of all the blessed Trinity. In that sight I saw and understood these three aspects:
    the aspect of the Fatherhood,
    the aspect of the Motherhood,
    and the aspect of the Lordhood,
        in one God.

In our Father Almighty we have our protection and our bliss as
    regards our natural essence (which is ours by our creation from
    without beginning);

and in the Second Person, in understanding and wisdom, we have
    our protection as regards our fleshliness, our redeeming and our
    saving,
    for He is our Mother,
    Brother,
    and Savior.

And in our good Lord the Holy Spirit, we have our rewarding and
    our
    recompense for our living and our trouble—
    endlessly surpassing all that we desire,
    in His amazing courtesy, from His high plenteous grace.

For all our life is in three.
    In the first, we have our being;
    and in the second, we have our growing;
    and in the third, we have our completing.

The first is nature;
the second is mercy;
the third is grace.

As for the first: I saw and understood that
    the high Power of the Trinity is our Father,

and the deep Wisdom of the Trinity is our Mother,
and the great Love of the Trinity is our Lord; and all this we have
in our human nature and in our essential creation.

And furthermore, I saw that the Second Person, who is our Mother
in essence,
that same dearworthy Person has become our Mother in flesh.

For we are two-fold in God's creation: that is to say, essential
and fleshly.
Our essence is the higher part, which we have in our Father,
God Almighty;
and the Second Person of the Trinity
is our Mother in human nature in our essential creation. In
Him we are grounded and rooted,
and he is our Mother in mercy by taking on our fleshliness.

And thus our Mother is to us various kinds of actions
(in Whom our parts are kept unseparated)
for in our Mother Christ, we benefit and grow,
and in mercy He redeems and restores us,
and, by the virtue of His Passion and His death and
resurrection, He ones us to our essence.
In this way, our Mother works in mercy to all His children
who are submissive and obedient to Him.

And grace works with mercy, and namely in two properties as it
was shown (which working belongs to the Third Person,
the Holy Spirit). He works, rewarding and giving;
"rewarding" is a great gift of trust which the Lord gives to
him who has labored,
and "giving" is a gracious action which he does freely of
grace, fulfilling and surpassing all that is deserved by
creatures.

152

Thus in our Father, God Almighty, we have our being;
and in our Mother of mercy we have our redeeming and restoring,
in whom our parts are one-ed and all made complete man;
and by the repaying and giving in grace of the Holy Spirit, we are fulfilled.

And our essence is in our Father, God Almighty,
and our essence is in our Mother, God all Wisdom,
and our essence is in our Lord the Holy Spirit, God all Goodness,
for our essence is total in each Person of the Trinity, which is One God.

But our fleshliness is only in the Second Person, Christ Jesus
(in whom is the Father and the Holy Spirit)
and in Him and by Him we are mightily taken out of hell
and out of the misery on earth,
and honorably brought up into heaven
and full blessedly one-ed to our essence, increased in riches and nobility,
by all the virtue of Christ and by the grace and action of the Holy Spirit.

59

All this bliss we have by mercy and grace,
which kind of bliss we might never have had or known if the quality of goodness which is in God had not been opposed—
by which goodness we have this bliss.

For wickedness has been permitted to rise in opposition to that goodness, and the goodness of mercy and grace opposed against the wickedness, and transformed all into goodness and into honor for all those that shall be saved, for that is the quality in God which does good against evil.

Thus Jesus Christ who does good against evil is our true Mother—
we have our being from Him where the basis of motherhood begins,
with all the sweet protection of love that accompanies it endlessly.

As truly as God is our Father,
so truly God is our Mother.
   (And that He showed in all the showings, and
   particularly in those sweet words where he says
   "It is I"—that is to say:
   "It is I: the Power and the Goodness of the Fatherhood.
    It is I: the Wisdom of the Motherhood.
    It is I: the Light and the Grace that is all blessed Love.
    It is I: the Trinity.
    It is I: the Unity.
      I am the supreme goodness of all manner of things.
      I am what causes thee to love.
      I am what causes thee to yearn.
    It is I: the endless fulfilling of all true desires.")

For the soul is highest, noblest, and worthiest
   when it is lowest, humblest, and gentlest.

From this essential foundation we have
   all our virtues
   and our fleshliness
     by the gift of nature and
     by the help and assistance of mercy and grace, without which
       we cannot benefit.

Our high Father, God Almighty, who is Being itself, knew us and
loved us from before any time,
   and from this knowledge in His wondrous profound love, by the
   foreseeing endless agreement of all the Blessed Trinity,
   He willed that the Second Person should become our Mother, our
   Brother, and our Savior.

Whereof it follows that as truly as God is our Father,
so truly God is our Mother.
   Our Father wills,
   our Mother acts,
   our good Lord the Holy Spirit strengthens.

And therefore it is right for us
   to love our God in whom we have our being, reverently thanking
      and praising Him for our creation,
   powerfully praying to our Mother for mercy and pity,
   and to our Lord the Holy Spirit for help and grace, for in these
      three is all our life—nature, mercy, and grace—from which
      we get humility,
            gentleness,
            patience,
            and pity,
            and hatred of sin and wickedness
      (for it is right and proper for the virtuous to hate sin and
      wickedness).

Thus is Jesus our true Mother in nature,
   from our first creation,
and He is our true Mother in grace
   by His taking our created human nature.

All the fair action and all the sweet natural function of dearworthy
motherhood is attached to the Second Person; for in Him we have
this divine will whole and safe without end, both in nature and grace,
from His own excellent goodness.

   I understood three ways of looking at motherhood in God:
      the first is the creating of our human nature;
      the second is His taking of our human nature (and there com-
         mences the motherhood of grace);
      the third is motherhood of action (and in that is a great reaching

155

outward, by the same grace, of length and breadth and of
height and of depth without end)
and all is one love.

60

But now it is appropriate to say a little more about this reaching
outward, as I understood it in the meaning of our Lord—
how that we are brought back by the Motherhood of mercy
and grace into the womb of our human nature where we
were created by the Motherhood of natural love, which
natural love never leaves us.

Our Mother in human nature, our Mother in grace—because He
wished to completely become our Mother in everything, He accepted
the foundation of His work most lowly and most mildly in the
Maiden's womb.

(And that He showed in the first showing, where he brought that
meek Maid before the eye of my understanding in the simple state
she was in when she conceived.)

That is to say, our high God, the supreme Wisdom of all, in this lowly
womb clothed Himself and enclosed Himself most willingly in our
poor flesh, in order that He Himself could do the service and the duty
of motherhood in everything.

The mother's serving is most near,
   most willing,
   and most certain
      ("near" because it is most of human nature; "willing," because
      it is most loving; and "certain," because it is most true).

This duty no one can, nor could, nor ever did to the fullest,
except He alone.

We are aware that all our mothers give us birth only to pain and dying; and what is it but that our true Mother Jesus, He—all love—gives us birth to joy and to endless life. Blessed may He be!

Thus He carries us within Himself in love, and labors until full term
    so that He could suffer the sharpest throes
        and the hardest pains that ever were
        or ever shall be,
        and die at the last.

And when He had finished, and so given us birth to bliss, not even all this could satisfy His wondrous love.
    (And that He showed in these high, surpassing words of love: "If I could suffer more, I would suffer more.")

He could die no more, but He would not cease working, therefore, it
    behooved Him that He feed us
(for the dearworthy love of motherhood has made Him owe us
    that).

The mother can give her child suck from her milk, but our precious Mother Jesus can feed us with Himself;
    and He does it most graciously and most tenderly with the Blessed Sacrament which is the Precious Food of true life.

    And with all the sweet Sacraments He supports us most mercifully and graciously.
        (And thus meant He in this blessed word where He said: "It is I that Holy Church preaches to thee and teaches to thee"; that is to say, "All the wholeness and life of Sacraments, all the virtue and grace of my Word, all the goodness that is ordained in Holy Church for thee, it is I.")

The mother can lay the child tenderly on her breast,
but our tender Mother Jesus can more intimately lead us *into* His blessed Breast by His sweet open Side,

and show therein part of the Godhead
and part of the joys of heaven,
    with spiritual certainty of eternal bliss.

(And that was shown in the tenth showing, giving the same
understanding in this sweet word where He says, "Lo, how I
love thee," gazing into His side and rejoicing.)

This fair lovely word "mother" is so sweet and so kind in itself, that
it can not truly be said of anyone nor to anyone except of Him and to
Him who is true Mother of life and of all.

To the quality of motherhood belongs natural love, wisdom, and
knowledge—and this is God;
    for though it is true that our bodily birth is but little, lowly, and
        simple as compared to our spiritual birth,
    yet it is He who does it within the created mothers by whom it is
        done.

The kind, loving mother who is aware and knows the need of her
child protects the child most tenderly as the nature and state of
motherhood wills.
    And as the child increases in age, she changes her method but not
        her love.
    And when the child is increased further in age, she permits it to
        be chastised to break down vices and to cause the child to
        accept virtues and graces.
This nurturing of the child, with all that is fair and good, our Lord
does in the mothers by whom it is done.

Thus He is our Mother in our human nature by the action of grace in
the lower part, out of love for the higher part.

    And He wishes us to know it; for He wishes to have all our love
        made fast to Him.

In this I saw that all our debt that we owe by God's bidding to fatherhood and motherhood (because of God's Fatherhood and Motherhood) is fulfilled in true loving of God which blessed love Christ works in us.

(And this was shown in all the showings and specifically in the high bountiful words where He says: "It is I whom thou lovest.")

61

In our spiritual birthing, our Mother uses more tenderness for our protection without any comparison
    (by as much as our soul is of more value in His sight than the flesh).
    He kindles our understanding,
    He directs our ways,
    He eases our conscience,
    He comforts our soul,
    He lightens our heart,
        and He gives us, partially, knowledge and love of His blessed Godhead—along with gracious remembrance of His sweet manhood and His blessed Passion,
        with gracious wonder at His high, surpassing goodness,
    and He makes us to love all that He loves because of His love, and to be satisfied with Him and all His works.

If we fall, quickly He raises us by His loving calling and merciful touching.

And when we are thus strengthened by His sweet action, then we willingly choose Him, by His sweet grace, to be His servants and His lovers everlastingly without end.

After this He permits some of us to fall more severely and more grievously than ever we did before, as it seems to us.

And then we believe (we who are not all-wise) that all was naught
that we had begun.
But it is not so,
because it is necessary for us to fall,
and it is necessary for us to see it.
For if we fell not, we would not know how weak and how
miserable we are by ourselves—nor also would we so
thoroughly know the amazing love of our Creator.

For we shall see truly in heaven without end that we have grievously
sinned in this life,
and, notwithstanding this, we shall see that we were never lessened
in His
love, nor were we ever of less value in His sight.
By means of the test of this falling,
we shall gain a high, wondrous knowledge of love in God
without end.
For strong and wondrous is that love which cannot nor will not
be broken because of trespass.
And this is one understanding of our benefits from falling.

Another is the lowliness and humility that we shall gain by the sight
of our falling,
for thereby we shall be highly raised in heaven
and we might never have come to this raising without that humility.
And therefore it is necessary for us to see our fall,
for if we see it not, though we fall, it would not benefit us.

And usually, first we fall, and afterwards we see it—and both by the
mercy of God.
The mother can allow the child to fall sometimes and to be distressed
in various ways for its own benefit, but she can never permit any
kind of peril to come to the child, because of her love.
But even if our earthly mother could allow her child to perish,

our heavenly Mother Jesus cannot allow us that are His children to
   perish.
He is all Power,
   all Wisdom,
      and all Love, and so is none but He. Blessed may He be!

But often when our falling and our misery is shown us, we are so
sorely frightened and so greatly ashamed of ourselves that scarcely
do we know where we can hide ourselves away.
   Then our courteous Mother wills not that we flee away—for Him
      nothing would be more distasteful—
   but He wills then that we follow the behavior of a child, for when
      a child is distressed or afraid, it runs hastily to the mother for
      help with all its might.
   So wishes He that we act as a humble child, saying thus: "My kind
      Mother, my gracious Mother, my dearworthy Mother, have
      mercy on me. I have made myself foul and unlike to Thee,
      and I am neither able nor know how to amend it except with
      Thy secret help and grace."

And if we do not feel ourselves eased very quickly, we may be
sure that He is practicing the behavior of a wise mother, for if He
sees that it would be more benefit to us to mourn and weep, out of
love He permits it with compassion and pity until the best time.

And He wills then that we practice the behavior of a child who
constantly naturally trusts to the love of the mother in well and woe.

And He wills that we betake ourselves strongly to the Faith of Holy
Church and find there our dearworthy Mother in the solace of true
understanding with all the Blessed Communion of Saints.

For one particular person can often be broken, as it seems, by
himself, but the whole Body of Holy Church is never broken, nor
ever shall be, without end.

161

And therefore a certain thing it is, a good and a gracious thing, to will humbly and strongly to be made fast and one-ed to our Mother, Holy Church, that is, Christ Jesus.
For the flood of mercy that is His dearworthy Blood and precious Water is adequate to make us fair and pure.
The blessed Wound of our Savior is open and rejoices to heal us.
The sweet gracious hands of our Mother are already and diligently about us.

For He in all this action practices the duty of a kind nurse who has nothing else to do except to attend to the safety of her child.

It is His function to save us,
it is His honor to do it,
and it is His will that we acknowledge it.

For He wills that we love Him sweetly
and trust in Him humbly and strongly.

(And this He showed in these grace-filled words: "I keep thee full safely.")

62

At that time He showed
   our frailty and our failings,
   our betrayals and our denials,
   our despisings and our burdens,
   and all our woes
      to whatever extent they could befall us in this life, as it seemed to me.

And along with that He showed
   His blessed Power,

His blessed Wisdom,
His blessed Love in which
He keeps us in these difficult times just as tenderly and as
sweetly for His honor and as surely for our salvation
as He does when we are in the most solace and comfort.

To do that He raises us spiritually and nobly into heaven, and
transforms all our woe into His honor and our joy without end.

His love never permits us to lose opportunity.

And all of this is from the natural goodness of God, by the working
of grace.

God is natural in His very being—
that is to say, that goodness which is of nature,
it is God.

He is the ground;
He is the essence;
He is the same thing as nature;
and He is true Father and true Mother of human nature.

All natures that He has caused to flow out of Him to accomplish His
will shall be returned and brought again into Him by the
salvation of man through the working of grace.
For of all natures that He has placed partially in various created
things, only in man is all the whole
in fullness,
in strength,
in beauty and in goodness,
in majesty and nobility,
in all manner of solemnity,
of preciousness,
and of honor.

Here we can see
    that we are fully bound to God because of our human nature,
    and we are also fully bound to God because of grace.

Here we can see that we need not intensely search
    far away to discover the different vital powers,
    but only as far as Holy Church—into our Mother's breast
        (that is to say, into our own soul, where our Lord dwells),
    and there we shall find everything—now in faith and belief, and
        afterwards, truly in Himself clearly, in bliss.

But let no man or woman take this exclusively to himself, for it is not
    so—it is general!

For it was our precious Mother Christ for whom this fair human
        nature was prepared,
    for the honor and nobility of man's creation,
    and for the joy and the bliss of man's salvation—just as He
        understood,
        knew,
        and recognized from without beginning.

63

Here we can see
    that we truly have it from our human nature to hate sin,
    and we truly have it from grace to hate sin—
        for human nature is all good and fair in itself,
        and grace was sent out
            to preserve human nature
            and to destroy sin
            and to bring back fair human nature
                to the blessed point from whence it came—
                that is, God—

with more nobility and honor
by the virtuous working of grace.

For it shall be seen before God in regard to all His holy saints in joy
without end
that human nature has been tested in the fire of tribulation and no
lack, no flaw found in it.

Thus are human nature and grace of one accord—
for grace is God
as human nature is God.
He is double in His way of working
but single in love,
and neither of these two works without the other,
nor is either separated from the other.

When we by the mercy of God and with His help come to harmony
with both our human nature and grace,
we shall see honestly that sin is truly more vile and more painful
than hell, without comparison,
for sin is opposite to our fair human nature!

For as truly as sin is impure,
just as truly is it unnatural,
and thus it is a horrible thing to see for the beloved soul that
wishes to be all fair and shining in the sight of God as both human
nature and grace direct.
But let us not be afraid of this (except in so much as fear could help
us); but humbly let us make our moan to our dearworthy Mother,
and He shall all besprinkle us with His Precious Blood
and make our souls very pliant and very gentle,
and restore us to health most gently in the course of time,
in whatever way as it is most honor to Him and most joy to us
without end.

He shall never cease this sweet, fair working, nor pause, until all His dearworthy children are birthed and brought forth.

(And He showed that where He showed the interpretation of spiritual thirst: that is, the love-longing that shall last until Doomsday.)

Thus in our true Mother, Jesus, our life is grounded,
   in His own foreseeing Wisdom from without beginning,
   with the high Power of the Father
   and the high supreme Goodness of the Holy Spirit.

In the taking of our human nature He restored life to us, and in His blessed dying upon the cross, He birthed us into endless life.

And from that time, and now, and until Doomsday,
   He feeds us and helps us
   just as the high matchless nature of motherhood wills
   and as the natural need of childhood requires.

Fair and sweet is our heavenly Mother in the eyes of our soul; precious and loving are His grace-filled children in the eyes of our heavenly Mother,
   with gentleness and humility and all the fair virtues that are proper to children in nature.

Furthermore,
   by nature the child does not despair of the mother's love;
   by nature the child does not take responsibility upon itself;
   by nature the child loves the mother
      and each one of them the other.

These are the fair virtues (with all others that are like them) with which our heavenly Mother is honored and pleased.

I recognized no state in this life
   greater in weakness,
   and in the lack of power and intelligence than our childhood,
until the time that our grace-filled Mother has brought us up to our
Father's bliss.

And then truly shall be made known to us His meaning in these sweet
words where Christ says:
   "All shall be well;
   and thou shalt see for thyself that all manner of things
      shall be well."

And then shall the bliss of our Motherhood in Christ be begun anew
   in the joys of our Father God
   and this new beginning shall continue being renewed without end.

Thus I understood that all His blessed children which have been
birthed from Him by nature shall be brought back into Him by grace.

64

Before this time, by the gift of God, I had a great yearning and desire
to be delivered from this world and from this life,
   for frequently I beheld the woe that is here,
   and the well and the bliss that exists there.

   And even if there had been no pain in this life except the
   absence of our Lord, it seemed to me that that was sometimes
   more than I could bear.

And this absence made me mourn and earnestly yearn—and also my
own misery, sloth, and weakness—so that I had no delight in living
or laboring as it fell to me to do.

To all this our gracious Lord answered for the sake of comfort and patience, and He said these words:

"Without warning thou shalt be taken
from all thy pain,
from all thy sickness,
from all thy distress,
and from all thy woe,
and thou shalt come up above,
and thou shalt have me for thy reward,
and thou shalt be filled full of love and bliss,
and thou shalt never have any manner of pain,
nor any manner of sickness,
nor any manner of displeasure,
nor any lack of will,
but always joy and bliss without end.
Why then should it bother thee to suffer awhile, seeing that it is my Will and to my honor?"

In this word: "Without warning thou shalt be taken . . . ," I saw that God rewards man for the patience that he has in awaiting God's will,
and for his lifetime (if that man extends his patience over the time of his life)
because of not knowing the time of his passing away.

This is a great benefit, for if a man knew the time of his passing, he would not have patience concerning that time.

Also God wills that while the soul is in the body, it seems to itself that it is always at the moment of being taken.

For all this life and this languishing that we have here is only a moment, and when we are taken without warning out of pain into bliss, then the pain shall have been nothing.

168

At this time I saw a body lying on the earth
　　which appeared thick and ugly and fearsome,
　　without shape and form,
　　as it were a bloated heap of stinking mire.

And suddenly out of this body sprang a most fair creature,
　　a tiny child,
　　well-shaped and formed,
　　quick and lively,
　　whiter than a lily,
　　　which neatly glided up into heaven.
　The bloatedness of the body symbolizes the great misery of our
　　　mortal flesh,
　　and the tinyness of the child symbolizes the clearness and purity of
　　　our soul.

And I considered:
　　"With this body remained none of the fairness of the child,
　　nor on this child did there remain any foulness of the body."

It is most blessed for man to be taken from pain,
more than for pain to be taken from man;
　　for if pain is taken from us, it can come again.
Therefore is it an unequalled comfort and a blessed awareness for a
loving soul that we shall be taken from pain,
　　for in this promise I saw
　　　a merciful compassion that our Lord has to us in our woe and a
　　　gracious promise of pure deliverance,
for He wills that we be comforted in surpassing joy.

　　　(And that He showed in these words:
　　　"And thou shalt come up above;
　　　and thou shalt have me for thy reward;
　　　and thou shalt be filled full of joy and bliss.")

169

It is God's will that we fix the point of our concentration on this blessed sight as often as we can and for as long a time as we can keep ourselves therein with His grace.

For this is a blessed contemplation for the soul that is guided by God and very much to its honor for the time that it lasts.

And when we fall again into ourself
   by sluggishness and spiritual blindness
   and the experiencing of spiritual and bodily pains
      because of our frailty,
it is God's will that we recognize that He has not forgotten us.

     (And this He means in these words He says for the sake of comfort: "And thou shalt never more have pain, nor any manner of sickness, nor any manner of displeasure, nor lack of will, but ever joy and bliss without end. Why should it bother thee to suffer awhile seeing that it is my will and to my honor?")

It is God's will
   that we accept His promises and His comfortings
   as broadly and as powerfully as we can receive them.
And He also wills
   that we accept our waiting and our distress
   as lightly as we can take them, and pay no attention to them—
      for the more lightly we take them,
       and the less value we place on them for the sake of love,
         the less pain shall we have in experiencing them,
          and the more favor and reward will we have because of them.

65

Thus I understood that whatever man or woman willingly chooses God in this life for the sake of love, he can be certain that he is loved without end with endless love which creates in him that grace.

He wills that we hold on to this trustfully—
    that we are all in as certain hope of the bliss of heaven
        while we are here,
    as we shall be in certainty when we are there.

And the more delight and joy that we take in this certainty with
reverence and humility, the better it pleases Him, as it was shown.
    This reverence that I mean is a holy, gracious fear of our Lord,
    to which humility is knit:
        and that is, that a creature sees
            the Lord as wondrous great,
            and the self as wondrous small.

For these virtues are possessed eternally by the beloved God, and
this can be understood and experienced now in some measure by the
presence of our Lord when that presence occurs.
    This presence in everything is most desired,
        because it produces wondrous reassurance,
        in true faith and certain hope by the greatness of love,
        in fear that is sweet and delightful.

It is God's will that I see myself just as much bound to Him in love
as if He had done all that He has done just for me.
    And thus should every soul think in regards to His Love: that is
        to say, the love of God creates in us such a unity that when
        it is truly understood, no man can separate himself from
        any other.
And thus ought our soul to understand that God has done just for
itself all that He has done.

This He shows in order to make us love Him and fear nothing but
    Him; for it is His will that we be aware that all the power of
    the Enemy is held in our Friend's hand.

Therefore the soul that surely recognizes this shall fear nothing
except Him whom it loves.

171

All other fears the soul reckons along with passions and bodily sickness and fantasies, and therefore, although we may be in so much pain, woe, and distress that it seems to us that we can think of absolutely nothing except what we are in or what we are experiencing, as soon as we can, we pass lightly over it and we set it at nought.

And why? Because we know God's wish that
  if we know Him
  and love Him
  and reverently fear Him,
    we shall have peace and be in great repose,
    and all that He does shall be a great pleasure to us.

  (And this showed our Lord in these words: "Why should it bother thee to suffer awhile, since it is my will and to my honor?")

Now I have told you of fifteen revelations as God granted to deliver them to my mind,
  renewed by enlightenings and inspirations
  (I hope, from the same Spirit who showed them all).

Of these fifteen showings the first began early in the morning, about the hour of four, and they lasted, appearing in a most beautiful order and solemnly, each following the other, until it was three in the afternoon or later.

66

After this, the good Lord showed the sixteenth showing on the following night, as I shall say later,
and the sixteenth was the conclusion and confirmation of all fifteen.

Except first it behooves me to tell you about my weakness, misery, and blindness.

I have said in the beginning, "And in this all my pain was suddenly taken from me." From this pain I had no grief and no distress as long as the fifteen showings lasted one after another, and at the end all was concealed and I saw no more.

And soon I sensed that I would live and linger on, and immediately my sickness came again—first in my head, with a sound and a noise, and without warning all my body was filled full of sickness just as it had been before, and I was so barren and so dry that I had but little comfort.

And as a wretch I moaned gloomily because of the experience of my bodily pains, and for the lack of comfort, spirtually and bodily.

Then a member of a religious order came to me and asked how I fared.

And I said that I had been raving today, and he laughed aloud and inwardly.

I said, "The cross that stood before my face, it seemed to me that it bled profusely."

And with this word, the person that I spoke to grew all serious and marveled.

And immediately I was sore ashamed and amazed at my recklessness, and I thought,

"This man takes seriously the least word that I could say" and then I saw no more of him.

But when I saw that he took it seriously and with such great respect, I grew most greatly ashamed,

and I would have been shriven,

except at that time I could tell it to no priest,

for I thought, "How would a priest believe me when, by saying I raved, I showed myself not to believe our Lord God?"

173

(even though I believed Him truly during the time that I saw Him, and so was then my will and my intention to do so forever without end—but, like a fool, I let it pass from my mind).

Ah, behold me, a wretch!
This was a great sin, a great unkindness, that I, out of folly, out of feeling a little bodily pain, so stupidly lost for the time the comfort of all this blessed showing of our Lord God.

Here you can see what I am by myself.

But even in this our gracious Lord would not leave me.
And I lay still until night, trusting in His mercy,
    and then I began to sleep.

In my sleep, at the beginning, it seemed that the Fiend fixed on my throat, thrusting forth a face like a young man's very near to my face; and the face was long and wondrous thin. I never saw any such.
The color was red like the tilestone when it is new fired, with black spots in it like black holes, fouler than tilestone.
His hair was red as rust, clipped off in front, with side locks hanging on the temples.
He snarled at me with an evil expression, showing white teeth, and so much that I thought it even more repulsive.
He had no fit body nor hands, but with his paws he held me by the throat and would have strangled me, but he could not.

(This horrible showing was given in sleep, as was no other.)

And during all this time,
I trusted to be saved and protected by the mercy of God.
And our gracious Lord gave me grace to awaken,
    and scarcely had I any life.

174

The persons that were with me watched me and wet my temples,
and my heart began to relax.

Immediately a little smoke came in the door with a great heat and a
foul stink.
I said, "*Benedicite domine!* Everything here is on fire!"
And I imagined that it was a physical fire that would have burnt
us all to death.

I asked those who were with me if they sensed any odor.
They said no, they smelled none.
I said, "Blessed be God!"
because then I was well aware that it was the Fiend that had
come only to tempt me.

And immediately I betook myself to what our Lord had shown me on
that same day,
with all the Faith of Holy Church
(for I look upon them as both the same),
and I fled to that as to my comfort.

And soon all vanished away,
and I was brought to great repose and peace
without sickness of body or fear of conscience.

67

And then our Lord opened my spiritual eye and showed me my soul
in the midst of my inner self.

I saw my soul as large
as if it were an endless castle
and as if it were a blessed kingdom;

and by the circumstances I saw in it
   I understood that it is an honorable City.

   In the midst of that City sits our Lord Jesus Christ,
      true God and true man,
      a handsome person,
      and of tall stature,
         a most exalted Bishop,
         a most solemn King,
         a most honorable Lord.

And I saw Him arrayed with great pomp and honor.
   He sits in the soul calmly upright in peace and repose, and He
   rules and guards heaven and earth and all that exists.

The Manhood sits with the Godhead in repose,
and the Godhead rules and guards without any agent or activity.
And the soul is all occupied with the blessed Godhead, who is
      supreme Power,
   supreme Wisdom,
   and supreme Goodness.

The place that Jesus takes in our soul,
   He will never move it away forever, as I see it, for in us is His
   most familiar home and His eternal dwelling.

And in this He showed the delight that He has in the creating
      of man's soul
   —for as well as the Father had the power to make a creature,
   and as well as the Son had the knowledge to make a creature,
   equally well did the Holy Spirit have the wish that man's soul be
      made;
   and so it was done.

And therefore the blessed Trinity rejoices without end in the creating
of man's soul,

for He saw from without beginning
what would please Him without end.

Everything that He has made shows His Lordship.

An understanding was given at the same time by the illustration
of a creature that was led to see great nobility and kingdoms
belonging to a lord, and when he had seen all the nobility below,
then, marveling, he was moved to go above to the high place
where the lord dwells, knowing by reason that his dwelling is in
the most honorable place.

And thus I understood truly that our soul can never have rest in
things that are beneath itself.
And when it comes above all created things into the self, still it
cannot remain in the contemplation of the self, but all its
contemplation is blissfully fixed on God who is the Creator
dwelling in the self (for in man's soul is His true dwelling).

The highest light and the brightest shining of the City is the glorious
love of our Lord, as I see it.

And what can make us rejoice in God more than to see in Him that
He rejoices in us, the highest of all His works?

For I saw in the same showing
    that if the blessed Trinity could have made man's soul any better,
        any more beautiful, any nobler than it was made,
    He would not have been wholly pleased with the creation of man's
        soul.

But because He made man's soul as fair, as good, as precious a
creature as He could make it,
    therefore the Blessed Trinity is wholly pleased without end in the
        creation of man's soul,

and He wills that our hearts be powerfully raised above the depths
of the earth and all vain sorrows,
and rejoice in Him.

68

This was a delightful sight and a restful showing that is without end,
and the contemplation of this while we are here,
that is most pleasant to God
and very great help to us.

And the soul that thus contemplates it makes itself to be like Him
who is contemplated, and ones itself in rest and peace by His grace.

It was a particular joy and bliss to me that I saw Him *seated,* because
the steadiness of sitting suggests endless dwelling.

And He gave me knowledge truthfully that it was He who showed
me everything before,
for when I had watched this,
with time for consideration,
then our good Lord revealed words most humbly
without voice and without opening of lips,
just as He had done before,
and said most sweetly:
"Be well aware that it was no raving that thou sawest today,
but accept it,
and believe it,
and keep thyself in it
and comfort thyself with it
and trust thyself to it,
and thou shalt not be overcome."

These last words were said to teach true certainty that it is our Lord
Jesus who showed me everything.

And just as in the first word that our good Lord revealed, referring
     to His blessed Passion: "With this is the Devil overcome"—
just so He said in this last word with completely true faithfulness,
     referring to us all: "Thou shalt not be overcome."

And all this teaching and this true comfort is universal for all my
fellow Christians as was said before—and this is God's will.

These words: "Thou shalt not be overcome," were said very sharply
and very powerfully, for certainty and comfort against all tribulations
that can come.

   He said not
        "Thou shalt not be tempted;
        thou shalt not be troubled;
        thou shalt not be distressed,"
     but He said,
        "Thou shalt not be overcome."

God wills that we take heed to these words,
and that we be very strong in certain trust,
in well and in woe,
     for as He loves and delights in us,
     so He wills that we love Him and delight in Him
        and strongly trust in Him;
        and all shall be well.

And soon after all was concealed, and I saw no more.

69

After this the Fiend came again with his heat and with his stink, and
made me most anxious.
   The stink was so vile and so painful,
   and the physical heat was fearful and troublesome also.

Also I heard a physical chattering as if it had been from two bodies, and both, it seemed to me, chattered at one time as if they were holding a parliament with a great business; and all was soft muttering, since I understood nothing that they said.

All this was to move me to despair, as I thought, seeming to me that
they ridiculed the saying of prayers
(as when prayers are said coarsely with the mouth, without the devout intention and wise effort which we owe to God in our prayers).

Our Lord God gave me grace to trust in Him,
and to comfort my soul with physical speech
as I would have done to another person who had been troubled.
(It seemed to me that their carryings-on could not be agreeable to any physical activity of mine.)

My physical eye I fixed upon the same cross where I had been in
comfort before that time,
my tongue I occupied with speaking of Christ's Passion and reciting
the Faith of Holy Church,
and my heart I made fast to God with all my trust and with all my
might.

And I thought to myself, saying:
"Thou hast now a great duty to keep thyself in the Faith in order that thou shouldst not be seized by the Enemy;
if thou wouldst now from this time onward be as busy to keep thyself from sin, this would be a good and a most excellent occupation,"
for it seemed that if I were truly safe from sin, I would be completely safe from all the fiends of hell
and the enemies of my soul.

And so he occupied me all that night, and in the day until it was
about six in the morning.

And immediately they were all gone,
all passed away,
and they left nothing but the odor;
and that still lasted awhile.

I scorned that Fiend, and so was I delivered from him by the virtue
of Christ's Passion, for with that is the Fiend overcome, as our
Lord Jesus Christ said before.

70

In all this blessed showing, our good Lord gave me understanding
that the vision would pass (which blessed showing the Faith holds to)
with His own good will and His grace,
for He left with me neither sign nor token by which I could know
this, but He left with me His own blessed word in true understanding, bidding me most powerfully that I should believe it.
And so I do!

Blessed may He be!

I believe that He is our Savior who showed it,
and that it is the Faith that He showed.

And therefore I believe it, rejoicing; and to it I am bound by all His
own intention, with these next words that follow: "Keep thyself
therein and comfort thyself with it and trust thyself to it."

Thus I am bound to maintain it in my Faith.

For on the same day that it was shown, as soon as the vision was
passed, like a wretch I forsook it and openly said that I had raved.

Then our Lord Jesus of His mercy would not let the vision perish,
but He showed it all again within my soul,

with more fullness,
with the blessed light of His precious Love,
saying these words most strongly and most humbly:

"Know it with certainty now that it was no raving that thou sawest
this day."
    As if He had said:
        "Because the vision was passed from thee, thou didst let it go
        and knew not how to preserve it; but know it now, that is to say,
        now that thou dost understand it."

This was said not only for that particular time,
but also to fix it there upon the foundation of my Faith
where He says immediately following:
    "But accept it, believe it, and keep thyself in it and comfort thyself
    with it and trust thyself to it; and thou shalt not be overcome."

In those six words which follow where He says "accept it . . . ,"
His intention is truly to make this fast in our heart,
    for He wills that it dwell with us in Faith until our life's end,
        and afterwards in fullness of joy,
            willing that we always have certain trust in His blessed prom-
                ises,
        knowing His goodness.

For our Faith is opposed in various ways by our own blindness and by
        our spiritual Enemy, within and without,
    and therefore our Precious Lover helps us with spiritual insight
        and
    true teaching in equally different ways, within and without,
        by which we can know Him.

And therefore in whatever manner He teaches us,
    He wills that we perceive Him wisely,
        receive Him sweetly,

and keep ourselves in Him full of faith—
for *beyond* the Faith is no goodness preserved in this life,
  as I see it,
and *below* the Faith is no health for souls,
but *in* the Faith there the Lord wills that we maintain ourselves.

For we must by His goodness and His own working maintain
  ourselves in the Faith,
and by His permitting it, we are tested in the Faith by spiritual
  opposition and made strong.

If our Faith had no opposition, it would deserve no reward, as far as
the understanding I have of all our Lord's meaning.

71

Glad and merry and sweet is the blessed loving face our Lord turns
to our souls;
  for He sees us always living in love-longing,
  and He wills that our soul be of glad expression to Him
  in order to give Him His reward.

And thus I hope with His grace that He has—and shall even more—
draw in our outer expression to the inner demeanor and make us all
at one with Him and each of us with the other, in the true lasting joy
that is Jesus.

I understand three kinds of expressions from our Lord.
  The first is the face of passion as He showed it while He was here
    in this life, dying. (Though this sight is mournful and sorrow-
    ful, yet it is also glad and merry, for He is God.)
  The second kind of face is pity and sympathy and compassion; and
    this He shows to all His lovers who have need of His mercy,
    with certainty of saving.

The third is the full blessed face as it shall be without end; and
this was continued most often and longest.

And thus
in the time of our pain and our woe,
He shows us the face of His Passion and of His cross,
helping us to bear it by His own blessed strength.

And in the time of our sinning,
He shows us the face of compassion and pity,
mightily protecting us and defending against all our enemies.

(And these two are the usual faces which He shows to us in
this life; with them mixing the third.)

And this third is His blessed face, partially like what it will be in
heaven.
And that face is a gracious inspiration and sweet enlightening of
the spiritual life by which we are saved in certain faith, hope
and love, with contrition and devotion and also with contemplation and all manner of true solace and sweet comforts.
The blessed face of our Lord God accomplishes that inspiring
and enlightening in us by grace.

72

But now it behooves me to tell how I saw mortal sin in those
creatures who shall not die because of sin, but live in the joy of God
without end.

I saw that two opposites should never be together in one place. The
greatest opposites that exist are the highest bliss and the deepest
pain.
The highest bliss that is is to have God in the radiance of endless
life,

seeing Him truly,
experiencing Him sweetly,
all peacefully enjoying Him in fullness of joy.
    (And thus was the blessed face of our Lord shown, but only
    partially.)

In this showing I saw that sin is most opposite to this, to such an
    extent that as long as we are mixed up with any part of sin,
    we shall never see clearly the blessed face of our Lord. And
    the more horrible and the more grievous our sins are, the
    deeper distance are we from this blessed sight for that time.

Therefore it seems to us frequently that we are in peril of death,
    in some part of hell,
    because of the sorrow and pain that the sin is for us.

And thus we are deadened for the time
    from the very sight of our blessed life.

But in all this I saw truthfully that we are not dead in the sight of
    God,
    nor does ever He pass away from us,
    but He shall never enjoy His full bliss in us
    until we enjoy our full bliss in Him,
    truly seeing His fair, blessed face,
        for we are ordained to that in nature,
        and get to it by grace.

Thus I saw how sin is mortal for only a short time in the blessed
creatures of endless life.

And ever the more clearly that the soul sees this blessed face by
    grace of loving, the more it yearns to see it in fullness;
for notwithstanding that
    our Lord God dwells in us

and is here with us,

and calls us

and enfolds us for tender love so that He can never leave us,

and is nearer to us than tongue can tell or heart can think, yet we can never cease moaning nor weeping nor yearning until the time when we look at Him clearly in His blessed face; for in that precious, blessed sight there can remain no woe nor any lack of well-being.

In this I saw cause for mirth and cause for mourning:

cause for mirth because our Lord our Creator is so near to us and within us, and we in Him, by the faithfulness of His great goodness in protecting us;

cause for mourning, because our spiritual eye is so blind and we are so borne down by the burden of our mortal flesh and the darkness of sin that we cannot look our Lord God clearly in His fair blessed face.

No, and because of this murkiness, scarcely can we even believe and trust His great love and His faithful protection of us.

That is why I say that we can never cease mourning nor weeping.

This "weeping" does not wholly signify pouring out of tears by our physical eyes, but also intends more spiritual interpretation,

for the natural desire of our soul to see His face is so great and so immeasurable that if all the splendor that ever God made in heaven and on earth were given to us for our solace, but we saw not the fair, blessed face of Himself, still we would not cease from mourning nor from spiritual weeping (that is to say, out of painful yearning) until the time we truly see the fair, blessed face of our Creator.

And if we were in all the pain that heart can think and tongue can tell, if we could at that time see His fair, blessed face, all this pain would not bother us.

186

Thus is this blessed sight the end of all manner of pain to the loving soul, and the fulfillment of all manner of joy and bliss.

(And that He showed in the high, wondrous words where He said, "I am He who is highest; I am He who is lowest; I am He who is all.")

It is proper for us to have three kinds of knowledge:
the first is that we know our Lord God;
the second is that we know ourselves, what we are by Him in nature and grace;
the third that we know humbly what we ourselves are as regards our sin and our weakness.

And the whole showing was given for these three, as I understand it.

73

All this blessed teaching of our Lord God was shown in three parts: that is to say,
by bodily sight,
and by word formed in my understanding,
and by spiritual insight.
As for the bodily sight, I have told it as I saw as truly as I can;
and as for the words, I have spoken them just as our Lord showed them to me;
and as for the spiritual insight, I have said somewhat, but I can never fully relate it, and therefore I am moved to say more about this insight (as God wills to give me grace).

God showed two kinds of sickness of soul that we have:
the one is impatience or sloth (for we bear our labor and our pains gloomily);
the other is despair or doubtful fear (as I shall say later).

In general, He showed sin with which everyone is involved, but in
particular He showed none but these two sins.

And these two are those which most trouble and tempt us (according
to what our Lord showed me),
from which He wills that we be put right.

> (I speak of such men and women who because of God's love
> hate sin and dispose themselves to do God's will; then by our
> spiritual blindness and our bodily gloom, we are most inclined
> to these sins, and therefore, it is God's will that they be known
> and then we shall refuse them as we do other sins.)

For help against this, full humbly our Lord showed
the patience that He had in His cruel Passion,
and also the rejoicing and the delight that He has from that
Passion because of love.

And this showed by example that we should gladly and wisely bear
our pains, for that is greatly pleasing to Him
and endless benefit for us.

And the cause why we are troubled with these sins is because of our
ignorance of Love,
for though the three Persons in the Trinity are all equal in
themselves, the soul received most understanding in Love;

yea, and He wills that in everything we have our contemplation and
our enjoyment in Love.

To this knowledge we are most blind;
for some of us believe
that God is all Power and is able to do all,
and that He is all Wisdom and knows how to do all,
but that He is all Love and *will* do all, there we stop.

This ignorance is that which most hinders God's lovers, as I see it,
for when we begin to hate sin and amend ourselves by the
command of Holy Church,
still there persists a fear that hinders us,
because of paying attention to ourselves and the sins
we have done in the past
(and some of us because of our present every-day sins),
for we keep not our covenants
nor maintain the purity in which our Lord places us,
but we fall frequently in so much misery that it is shame to
see it.
And the recognition of this makes us so sorry and so sorrowful
that scarcely do we know how to find any comfort.
And this fear we mistake sometimes for a humility, but this is
a shameful blindness and a weakness.
And we do not know to despise it as we do another sin which
we recognize (which comes through lack of true judgement) and it is against truth, for of all the properties of
the blessed Trinity, it is God's will that we have most
certainty and delight in Love.

For Love makes Power and Wisdom wholly submissive to us;
for just as by the graciousness of God He forgives our sin after the
time that we repent us,
just so He wills that we forgive our own sin in regard to our
unreasonable sorrow and our doubtful fears.

74

I understand four kinds of fear.

One is the fear of fright which comes to a man suddenly through
weakness. This fear does good, because it helps to purge man
(as does bodily sickness or such other pain which is not sin), for
all such pains help man if they are patiently taken.

The second is fear of pain by which a man is stirred and awakened
from the sleep of sin; for man that is hard asleep in sin is not
able, for the time, to perceive the gentle comfort of the Holy
Spirit until he has understanding of this fear of pain, of bodily
death, and of spiritual enemies. And this fear stirs us to seek the
comfort and mercy of God; and thus this fear helps us as an
entry place, and enables us to have contrition by the blessed
inspiration of the Holy Spirit.
The third is doubtful fear. Doubtful fear, in so far as it draws us to
despair, God wills to have transformed in us into love by true
acknowledgment of Love; that is to say, that the bitterness of
doubt be turned into the sweetness of natural love by grace; for
it can never please our Lord that His servants doubt His
Goodness.
The fourth is reverent fear, for there is no fear in us that fully
pleases God except reverent fear; and this is most gentle, for
the more of it one has, the less it is felt because of the sweetness
of love.

Love and fear are brothers;
    and they are rooted in us by the Goodness of our Creator
    and they shall never be taken from us without end.

We have it from our human nature to love
and we have it from grace to love;
    and we have it from human nature to fear
    and we have it from grace to fear.

It is part of the Lordship and of the Fatherhood to be feared,
as it is part of the Goodness to be loved;
    and it is as proper for us who are His servants and His children to
        fear Him for His Lordship and His Fatherhood,
    as it is proper for us to love Him for His Goodness.

And although this reverent fear and love are not separated, yet they are not both the same, but they are two in character and in operation (but neither of them can be had without the other).

Therefore I am certain that he who loves, fears—
even though he feels it only a little.

All fears other than reverent fear that are offered to us, although they come under the pretense of holiness, yet are not as true; and by this can they be known apart:
  that fear which makes us quickly to flee from all that is not good
      and fall onto our Lord's breast
      as the child into the mother's arms,
    with all our intention and with all our mind acknowledging our
      weakness and our great need,
    recognizing His everlasting Goodness and His blessed Love,
    seeking only Him for salvation,
    cleaving to Him with certain trust—
the fear which brings us into this process is natural, merciful,
good and true.
  And all that opposes this, either it is wrong, or it is mixed up with
    wrong.

Then this is the remedy—to know them both and refuse the wrong.

For the natural benefit that we have in this life from fear
    (by the merciful action of the Holy Spirit)
that same benefit will be in heaven before God, noble, gracious,
    and totally delightful.
And thus we shall in love be intimate and near to God, and we shall
    in fear be noble and gracious to God; and both equally.

We desire of our Lord God
  to fear Him reverently
  and to love Him humbly

191

and to trust Him mightily;
>for when we fear Him reverently and love Him humbly,
>our trust is never in vain;
>for the more that we trust—
>and the more strongly that we trust—
>the more we please and honor our Lord in whom we trust.

If we lack this reverent fear and humble love (as God forbid we should) our trust shall soon be misdirected for that period of time.

Therefore we much need to beseech our Lord for grace that we may
>have this reverent fear and humble love as His gift,
>in heart and in deed—
>for without this no man can please God.

75

I saw that God can do all that we need; and these three which I shall
>say we need:
>love,
>yearning,
>and pity.
>>Pity in love protects us in the time of our need, and yearning in
>>the same love draws us into heaven.

For the thirst of God is to have the whole of mankind within Himself;
in this thirst,
>He has drawn and drunken His Holy Souls who are now in bliss;
>and, gathering in His living members,
>He continually draws and drinks,
>and still He thirsts and yearns.

I saw three kinds of yearning in God (and all for one purpose), of
>which we have the same in us
>(and of the same strength and for the same purpose).

The first is that He yearns to teach us to know Him and to love
Him for ever, since that is suitable and advantageous to us.
The second is that He yearns to have us up into His bliss as souls
are when they are taken out of pain into heaven.
The third is to fill us with bliss; and that shall be completed on the
Last Day to last for ever.

For I saw (as it is known in our Faith) that the pain and sorrow shall
be ended for all that shall be saved.
And not only shall we receive the same bliss that souls have had in
heaven before,
but also we shall receive a new bliss, which shall be abundantly
flowing out of God into us and filling us up.

These are the good things which He has prepared to give us from
without beginning.
These good things are treasured and hidden in Himself, for until
that time, a created being is not strong or worthy enough to
receive them.

In this we shall see truly the reason for everything He has done,
and, even more,
we shall see the reason for all things that He has permitted.

And the bliss and the fulfillment shall be so deep and so high
that out of wonder and amazement
all created beings shall have for God so great a reverent fear
(surpassing what has been seen and felt before)
that the pillars of heaven shall tremble and quake.

But this kind of trembling and fear shall have no pain—rather it is
part of the noble majesty of God to be seen this way by His creatures,
fearfully trembling and quaking,
for abundance of joy endlessly marveling at the greatness of God
the Creator, and at the smallness of all that is made,

for the sight of this makes the creature wondrous humble and
   subdued.

Wherefore God wills (and it is also proper to us both in nature and
   grace) that we be aware and know of this experience, desiring
   this sight and this deed,
for it leads us in the right way
and preserves us in true life and ones us to God.

God is as great as He is good;
   and as much as it is part of His Goodness to be loved,
   equally much it is part of His Greatness to be feared;
      for this reverent fear is the fair courtliness that is in heaven
         before God's face.

And just as much as He shall then be known and loved far more than
   what He is now,
to the same extent He shall be feared far more than what He is now.

Therefore it is inevitable that all heaven and earth shall tremble and
quake when the pillars of heaven shall tremble and quake.

76

I speak but little of reverent fear, for I hope it can be understood in
this previous matter, but I am well aware that our Lord showed me
no souls except those that fear Him.

I am also well aware that the soul that truly accepts the teaching of
the Holy Spirit, hates sin more for its vileness and horribleness than
it does all the pain that is in hell.

For the soul that beholds the good nature of our Lord Jesus, hates
not hell, but sin, as I see it.

And therefore it is God's will that we recognize sin, and pray diligently and labor willingly, and seek teaching humbly, so that we do not fall blindly into sin;

    and if we fall, that we rise quickly (for it is the worst pain that the soul can have to turn from God any time there is sin).

When other men's sins come to mind, the soul that wishes to be in
       repose shall flee from that as from the pain of hell, searching in
       God for remedy for help against it,
for the beholding of other men's sins
makes, as it were, a thick mist before the eye of the soul,
and we cannot for the time see the fairness of God
       (unless we can behold another's sins
       with contrition with him,
       with compassion on him,
       and with holy desire to God for him,
    for without this it troubles and tempts and hinders the soul that
beholds those sins).

    (This I understood in the showing about compassion.)

In this blessed showing of our Lord, I have an understanding of two opposites:
    the one is the most wisdom that any creature can do in this life;
    the other is the most folly.
       The wisdom is for a creature to act following the will and advice
       of his highest supreme Friend. This blessed Friend is Jesus;
       and it is His will and His advice that we bind ourselves with
       Him and fix ourselves intimately to Him ever more, in
       whatever state we are. For whether we are filthy or pure,
       we are always the same in His love. For well or for woe,
       He wills that we never flee from Him.

       However, because of our changeability within ourselves we fall
       frequently into sin. Then we have this by the guidance of

195

our Enemy, through our own folly and blindness; for they say thus: "Thou art well aware that thou art a wretch, a sinner, and also untrue; for thou keepest not thy covenant; thou dost promise our Lord frequently that thou wilt do better, and immediately afterwards, thou fallest into the same—especially into sloth, into the wasting of time" (for that is the beginning of sin, as I see it, and especially to the creatures who have given themselves to serve our Lord with inner contemplation of His blessed goodness).

And this makes us fearful to appear before our gracious Lord.

Then it is our Enemy who will set us back with his false fear concerning our sinfulness because of the pain with which he threatens us. It is his intention to make us so gloomy and so weary in this that we would forget the fair, blessed beholding of our everlasting Friend.

77

Our good Lord showed the enmity of the Fiend,
    by which I understood that everything that is in opposition to love
    and to peace, it is the Fiend and of his party.

We both must fall because of our weakness and our folly;
and we must rise to more joy
    because of the mercy and grace of the Holy Spirit.

And if our enemy wins anything from us by our falling
    (for it is his delight),
he loses many-fold more in our rising by love and humility.

This glorious rising is such great sorrow and pain to him for, because
    of the hate that he has for our soul, he burns continually in envy.
And all this sorrow that he wishes to make us have,
    it shall turn upon himself.

And it was because of this that our Lord scorned him;
and this made me laugh mightily.

This, then, is the remedy:
    that we be aware of our sinfulness
    and flee to our Lord,
        for ever the more quickly we do so,
        the more advantageous it is for us to be near Him.

And this is what we say in our intention:
    "I know well I have deserved an evil pain,
    but our Lord is all Power and can punish me mightily,
    and He is all Wisdom and knows how to punish me with reason,
    and He is all Goodness and loves me tenderly."

And in this awareness it is necessary that we remain, for it is a loving humility of a sinful soul (wrought by the mercy and grace of the Holy Spirit) when we will willingly and gladly accept the scourging and chastening that our Lord Himself wishes to give us.

(And the chastening shall be wholly tender and very gentle if we will only consider ourselves pleased with Him and with all His works.)

For the penance that man takes upon himself was not shown to me— that is to say, it was not shown in particular—
    but it was shown particularly and highly and with full lovely demeanor that we should humbly and patiently bear and suffer the penance that God Himself gives us, with remembrance of His blessed Passion.

For when we have remembrance of His blessed Passion, with pity and love, then we suffer with Him as His friends did who saw it

      (and this was shown in the thirteenth showing,
      near the beginning, where it speaks of pity).

For He says,
"Accuse not thyself overly much,
questioning if thy tribulation and thy woe is all because of thy
sinfulness;
for it is not my will that thou be gloomy or sorrowful
undiscerningly;
for I tell thee, whatsoever thou doest, thou shalt have woe.
And therefore I will that thou wisely recognize thy penance
which thou art in constantly,
and that thou dost humbly accept it for thy penance,
and thou shalt then truly understand that all thy living is
beneficial penance."

This earth is imprisonment,
and this life is penance,
and in this remedy He wills that we rejoice:
that our Lord is with us,
guarding us
and leading us into the fullness of joy—for it is an endless joy to
us in our Lord's purpose:
that He who shall be our bliss when we are there,
is our protector while we are here,
our way,
and our heaven
in true love
and certain trust.

(He gave understanding of this in all the showings, and
particularly in the showing of His Passion where he caused
me mightily to choose Him for my heaven.)

If we flee to our Lord, we shall be comforted;
if we touch Him we shall be made pure;
if we cleave to Him we shall be secure and safe
from all manner of peril.

For our gracious Lord wills that we be as friendly with Him as heart can think or soul can desire.

But beware that we take not so recklessly this friendliness that we refrain from courtesy; for while our Lord Himself is supreme friendliness, He is also as courtly as He is friendly, for He is true courtesy.

And the blessed creatures that shall be in heaven with Him without end, He wishes to have them like Himself in all things, for to be like our Lord perfectly, that is our true salvation and our complete bliss.

And if we do not know how we shall do all this, let us desire it from our Lord and He shall teach us, for that is His own delight and His honor.

Blessed may He be!

78

Our Lord of His mercy shows us our sin and our weakness by the sweet gracious light of Himself,

for our sin is so vile and so horrible that He of His courtesy will not show it to us except by the light of His grace and mercy.

It is His will that we have knowledge concerning four things:

the first is that He is our ground from whom we have all our life and our being;

the second, that He protects us mightily and mercifully at the time we are in our sin and among all our enemies who are most fierce against us

(and so much the more are we in greater peril because we give the enemy occasion for that and know not our own need);

the third is how courteously He protects us and lets us know when
we go amiss;
the fourth is how steadfastly He waits for us and does not change
His demeanor, for He wills that we be transformed and
one-ed to Him in love as He is to us.

Thus by this grace-filled knowledge
we can see our sin beneficially without despair
(for truly we need to see it)
and by that sight we shall be made ashamed of ourselves,
and our pride and presumption shall be broken down.

It truly behooves us to see that by ourselves we are just nothing but
sin and wretchedness.
And thus by the sight of the less which our Lord shows us,
the more which we do not see is diminished, for He of His courtesy
adjusts the sight to us
(for it is so vile and so horrible that we would not endure to
see it as it is).

And by this humble knowledge thus, through contrition and grace,
we shall be broken away from all things that are not our Lord,
and then shall our blessed Savior perfectly heal us and one us to
Himself.

This breaking and this healing our Lord means with reference to all
mankind,
for he that is highest and nearest to God, he can see himself sinful
and needy with me,
and I who am the least and the lowest of those that shall be saved,
I can be comforted along with him that is highest.
So has our Lord one-ed us together in love.

When He showed me that I would sin, because of the joy that I had
in beholding Him, I did not readily pay attention to that showing, and

our courteous Lord stopped then, and would not teach me further until He gave me grace and the will to pay attention.

From this I was taught that although we are nobly lifted up into
contemplation by the particular gift of our Lord,
yet it is necessary for us along with that to have knowledge and awareness of our sin and our weakness.

Without this knowledge we cannot have true humility,
and without this humility we cannot be saved.

And also I saw that we cannot get this knowledge from ourselves, nor from any of our spiritual enemies, for they do not will us very much good (for if it were by their will, we should not see our sin until our ending day).

Then we are much beholden to God that He will Himself out of love show our sin and weakness to us in time out of mercy and grace.

79

Also I had in this showing more understanding—when He showed me that I would sin, I applied it simply to my own individual self, for I was not otherwise stirred at that time,
but by the high, gracious comfort of our Lord which followed
afterwards, I saw that His meaning was for all mankind—that is
to say, all mankind which is sinful and shall be until the Last Day
(of which group I am a member, as I hope, by the mercy of God)—
for the blessed comfort that I saw is large enough for us all.

And here I was taught that I ought to see my own sin, and not other men's sins (unless it could be for the comfort and help of my fellow Christians).

201

Also in this same showing where I saw that I would sin, was I taught to be cautious of my own uncertainty,

for I am not aware of how I shall fall,

nor do I know the measure nor the greatness of my sin.

(For I fearfully wished to have known that,

but to that I received no answer.)

Also our gracious Lord, at the same time, showed me most certainly and powerfully the endlessness and the unchangeability of His love.

And also, by His great goodness and His grace inwardly guarding, that His love and that of our souls shall never be separated in two, without end.

Thus in this fear I have cause for humility that saves me from presumption;

and in the blessed showing of love I have cause for true comfort and joy that saves me from despair.

All this friendly showing of our gracious Lord is a loving lesson and a sweet, gracious teaching from Himself in the comforting of our soul.

For He wills that we know, by His sweetness and familiar loving, that all that we see or sense, within or without, which is in opposition to this is from the Enemy and not from God—

such as this: if we are moved to be more heedless of our living or the keeping of our hearts because we have knowledge of this plenteous love, then we need greatly to beware, for this inclination, if it comes, is untrue, and we ought greatly to hate it, for none of it has any similarity to God's will.

When we are fallen because of frailty or blindness,

then our gracious Lord inspires us,

stirs us,

and calls us;

202

and then He wills that we see our wretchedness
and humbly let it be acknowledged.

But He does not wish us to remain thus,
nor does He will that we busy ourselves greatly about accusing
ourselves,
nor does He will that we be full of misery about ourselves;
for He wills that we quickly attend to Him;
for He stands all alone and waits for us constantly, sorrowing
and mourning until we come,
and hastens to take us to Himself;
for we are His joy and His delight,
and He is our cure and our life.

(Though I say that He stands all alone, I leave out speaking of the
Blessed Company of heaven, and speak of His function and His
working here on earth, in respect to the circumstances of the
showing.)

80

By three things man is grounded in this life, and by these three God
is honored and we are aided, protected, and saved.

The first is the use of man's natural reason;
the second is the common teaching of Holy Church;
the third is the inner grace-filled working of the Holy Spirit;
and these three are all from one God.

God is the ground of our natural reason;
and God is the teaching of Holy Church;
and God is the Holy Spirit.

All are different gifts which He wills that we have great regard for and pay attention to, for these work in us constantly all together, and these are important things.

He wishes us to have knowledge of these things here as it were in an ABC—that is to say, that we have a little knowledge, of which we shall have fullness in heaven, and that is to further us.
We acknowledge in our Faith
    that God alone took our human nature
        and none but He;
and, furthermore,
    that Christ alone did all the works that are part of our salvation,
        and none but He;
and just so He alone acts now in the last end—that is to say,
    He dwells here with us and rules us
    and governs us in this life,
    and brings us to His bliss.

And this shall He do as long as any soul is on earth who shall come to heaven—to such an extent that if there were no such soul but one,
    He would be with that one all alone until He had brought it up
    to His bliss.

I believe and understand the ministration of angels as the priests relate it, but it was not shown to me,
    for He Himself is nearest and humblest,
    highest and lowest,
    and does all;
        and not only all that we need,
        but also He does all that is honorable for our joy in heaven.

Where I say that He awaits us, sorrowing and mourning, it means
    that all the true feeling that we have in ourselves in contrition
    and compassion,
    and all the sorrowing and mourning because we are not one-ed
    with our Lord,
and all such which is beneficial, it is Christ in us.

And though some of us sense it seldom, it passes never from Christ
until the time that He has brought us out of all our woe.

For love never allows Him to be without pity.

And whenever we fall into sin
and give up the remembrance of Him
and the protection of our own soul,
    then Christ alone takes care of the responsibility of us.
    And thus He stands sorrowing and mourning.

Then it is proper for us, for the sake of reverence and kindness,
to turn ourselves quickly to our Lord and not leave Him alone.

    He is here alone with us all—that is to say, only for us is He here.

And whenever I am alienated from Him by sin, despair, or sloth, then
    I allow my Lord to stand alone, in as much as He is in me—and
    so it goes with all of us who are sinners.

But though it is true that we act this way frequently,
    His goodness never allows us to be alone,
    but He is constantly with us,
    and He tenderly excuses us,
    and always shields us from blame in His sight.

81

Our good Lord showed Himself to His creature in various ways,
    both in heaven and in earth,
but I saw Him adopt no resting place except in man's soul.

    He showed Himself on earth in the sweet Incarnation
    and in His blessed Passion.

And in other ways He showed Himself on earth where I say:
"I saw God in a point."
And in other ways He showed Himself on earth thus, as it were on
pilgrimage: that is to say, He is here with us, leading us, and
shall be until the time He has brought us all to His bliss in
heaven.

He showed Himself reigning at different times, as I said before,
but primarily in man's soul.
He has adopted His resting place there and His honorable City,
out of which honorable throne He shall never rise
nor move away without end.

Wondrous and splendid is the place where our Lord dwells.

Therefore He wills that we pay attention to His grace-filled
inspiration, more rejoicing in His undivided love
than sorrowing in our frequent fallings.

For it is the most honor to Him of anything that we can do that we
live in our penance gladly and merrily because of His love,
for He looks upon us so tenderly that He sees all our living here to
be penance.

The natural yearning in us for Him is a lasting penance in us,
which penance He produces in us
and mercifully He helps us to bear it.

His love makes Him to yearn,
His wisdom and His truth with His rightfulness make Him to put
up with us here,
and this is the way He wants to look at it in us.

For this life is our natural penance and the highest, as I see it,
for this penance never goes from us

until the time that we are fulfilled
when we shall have Him for our reward.

And therefore He wills that we fix our hearts on the transition—that
is to say, from the pain that we feel into the bliss that we trust.

82

But here our gracious Lord showed the sorrowing and the mourning
    of the soul, meaning thus:
  "I am well aware that thou livest for my love,
  merrily and gladly suffering all the penance that can come to thee,
  but in as much as thou dost not live without sin, therefore thou art
      sad and sorrowful,
    but even if thou couldst live without sin, thou wouldst still suffer
        for the sake of my love
      all the woe,
      all the tribulation and distress that could come to thee.
  And that is true.
  But be not much bothered by sin that comes to thee
      against thy will."

Here I understood that the lord looks upon the servant with pity and
    not with blame,
for this passing life does not require that we live wholly without sin.

He loves us endlessly,
and we sin habitually,
  and He shows the sin to us most gently;
  and then we sorrow and mourn prudently,
    turning ourselves to the contemplation of His mercy,
    cleaving to His love and goodness,
    seeing that He is our medicine,
    aware that we do nothing but sin.

Thus by the humility that we get from the sight of our sin,
faithfully knowing His everlasting love,
thanking and praising Him, we please Him.
"I love thee and thou lovest me;
and our love shall never be divided in two,
and for thy benefit, I suffer."

And all this was shown in spiritual understanding,
He saying these words:
"I keep thee full safely."

By the great desire that I saw in our blessed Lord that we should
live in this way
(that is to say, in yearning and rejoicing, as all this lesson of
love shows)
by this desire I understood that all that is opposed to this is not
from Him, but from enmity, and He wills that we know it by the
sweet gracious light of this natural love.

If there is any such one alive on earth who is constantly kept from
falling, I know it not, for it was not shown me.

But this was shown:
that whether in falling or in rising
we are ever preciously protected in one love.
In the sight of God we do not fall;
in the sight of self, we do not stand—
and both of these are true as I see it, but the way our Lord
God sees it is the highest truth.

Then are we much bound to God
because He wills in this life to show us this high truth.

And I understood that while we are in this life, it is most helpful to
us that we see both of these at once;

for the higher point of view keeps us in spiritual solace and true
rejoicing in God,
and the other, that is, the lower point of view, keeps us in fear and
makes us ashamed of ourselves.

But our good Lord wills always that we see ourselves more from the
point of view of the higher
(but not give up knowledge of the lower)
until the time that we are brought up above,
where we shall have our Lord Jesus for our reward,
and will be filled full of joy and bliss without end.

83

I had a partial inspiration, vision, and sense of three properties of
God of which the strength and outcome of the whole revelation
consists
(and they were seen in every showing, and most particularly
in the twelfth where it was often said, "I am He"):

The properties are these:
life,
love,
and light.
In life is wondrous familiarity,
and in love is gentle courtesy,
and in light is endless kindness.

These three properties were seen in one Goodness,
to which Goodness my reason wished to be one-ed
and to cleave to it with all my might.

I beheld with reverent fear (and greatly marveling at the sight and
the feeling of the sweet harmony) that our reason is in God,

understanding that it is the highest gift that we have received, and
that it is grounded in human nature.

Our Faith is a light, naturally coming from our Endless Day—that is
our Father, God;
    in this light our Mother, Christ,
    and our good Lord the Holy Spirit
    lead us in this passing life.

This light is meted out prudently,
    faithfully remaining with us as we need it in the night.

  The light is the cause of our life;
  the night is the cause of our pain and of all our woe,
    on account of which woe we earn endless reward and
    favor from God,
  for we, with mercy and grace,
    willingly acknowledge and believe our light,
    walking in it wisely and mightily.

And at the end of woe,
suddenly our eye shall be opened
and in clarity of sight
our light shall be full.
This light is God our Creator
and the Holy Spirit
in Christ Jesus our Savior.

Thus I saw and understood that our Faith is our light in our night;
    and the light is God, our Endless Day.

84

This light is love,
    and the meting out of this light is done for us beneficially by the
        wisdom of God,

for neither is the light so bright that we can see clearly our
blessed Day,
nor is it completely barred from us,
but it is such a light in which we live rewardingly with toil,
earning the endless honor-filled favor of God.

(And this was seen in the sixth showing where He said,
"I thank thee for thy service and thy labor.")

Thus love keeps us in faith and hope;
and faith and hope lead us to love.

And at the end all shall be love.

I had three kinds of understandings on this light of love:
the first is love uncreated;
the second is love created;
the third is love given.
Love uncreated is God;
love created is our soul in God;
love given is virtue—
and that is the grace-filled gift of action,
in which we love God for Himself,
and ourselves in God,
and all that God loves,
for God's sake.

85

I marveled greatly at this vision,
for notwithstanding our stupid living and our blindness here,
yet endlessly our gracious Lord looks upon us in this struggle,
rejoicing.

And of all things,
    we can please Him best
        by wisely and truly believing that,
        and rejoicing with Him and in Him.

For as truly as we shall be in the bliss of God without end,
        praising Him and thanking Him,
just as truly we have been in the foresight of God loved and known
        in His endless purpose from without beginning.

In this love without beginning He made us,
and in the same love He protects us
and never allows us to receive harm
    by which our bliss might be lessened.

Therefore when the Judgement is given
and we are all brought up above,
then shall we clearly see in God
the secrets which are now hidden from us.

    Then shall none of us be moved to say in any way:
        "Lord, if it had been thus-and-so,
        then it would
        have been all well";

    but we shall say all in one voice:
        "Lord, blessed mayest Thou be!
        Because it is as it is; it is well.
        And now we see truly
        that everything is done
        as was Thine ordinance
        before anything was made."

86

This book is begun by God's gift and His grace,
but it is not yet completed, as I see it.

For the sake of love let us all pray
together with God's working—
thanking,
trusting,
rejoicing,
for thus would our good Lord be prayed to
(as is the understanding that I received in all His own
meaning, and in the sweet words where He says most merrily,
"I am the basis of thy praying").

Truly I saw and understood in our Lord's meaning that He showed it
because He wished to have it known more than it is,
and in this knowledge He will give us grace to love Him
and cleave to Him.

For He beholds His heavenly treasure with such great love on earth
that He wills to give us more light and solace in heavenly joy by
drawing our hearts from the sorrow and darkness
which we are in.

From the time that it was shown, I desired frequently to know what
our Lord's meaning was. And fifteen years after (and more) I was
answered in spiritual understanding, saying thus:
"Wouldst thou know thy Lord's meaning in this thing?
Be well aware:
love was His meaning.
Who showed it thee? Love.
What showed He thee? Love.
Why did He show it thee? For love.

Keep thyself in that love and thou shalt know and see more
of the same,
but thou shalt never see nor know any other thing therein
without end."

Thus was I taught that love was our Lord's meaning.
And I saw full certainly in this and in all the showings,
that before God made us, He loved us
and this love was never slackened
nor ever shall be.

In this love He has done all His works,
and in this love He has made all things beneficial to us,
and in this love our life is everlasting.

In our creation we had a beginning,
but the love in which He created us was in Him from without
beginning,
and in this love we have our beginning.

And all this we shall see in God without end,
which may Jesus grant us. Amen.

COLOPHON
(Attributed to the scribe)

Thus ends the revelation of love of the Blessed Trinity
showed by our Savior Christ Jesus
for our endless comfort and solace,
and also to rejoice in Him in this passing journey of life.
Amen, Jesus, Amen.

I pray Almighty God that this book does not come into the hands of
anyone except those who are His faithful lovers, and those that will
submit themselves to the Faith of Holy Church and obey the whole-

214

some interpretation and teaching of the men who are of virtuous life, settled age, and profound learning, for this revelation is high theology and high wisdom, wherefore it cannot survive with him who is slave to sin and to the Devil. And beware that thou not accept one thing after thine own inclination and preference and omit another, for that is the situation of an heretic. But accept each thing with the other and truly understand that all is in agreement with Holy Scripture and grounded in the same, and that Jesus, our true love, light, and truth, shall show this wisdom about Himself to all pure souls who with humility ask constantly. And thou to whom this book shall come, thank our Savior Christ Jesus highly and heartily that He made these showings and revelations for thee, and to thee, out of His endless love, mercy, and goodness, to be a safe guide and conduct to everlasting bliss for thee and for us—which may Jesus grant us. Amen.

Here end the sublime and wonderful Revelations
of the unutterable love of God in Jesus Christ,
vouchsafed to a dear lover of His and in
her to all His dear friends and
lovers, whose hearts, like
hers, do flame in the
love of our
dearest
Jesu.

A Lonely Sort of Acrobat:
NOTES BY THE TRANSLATOR

In commenting on the process of translation, Lydia Davis writes with painful accuracy: "The translator, a lonely sort of acrobat, becomes confused in a labyrinth of paradox, or climbs a pyramid of dependent clauses and has to invent a way down from it through his own language."[1] In my own experience, I have found this work of translation to be primarily priestly—i.e., how can I find the precise incantation which will transubstantiate the spirit of the original into the flesh of the language I wish it to have?

I have had three goals in this work:

1. To make more accessible to modern readers the thought and spirituality of Julian (which has often been found to be daunting in the alien density and convolutions of its literary presentation, in its countless unattributed pronouns, its arcane internal referencing, and its obscurely technical theological language);

2. To preserve for a modern public as much as possible of the "person" of that *homely* and *courteous* anchoress, whose style and quality, with its antique gentility, its self-effacement, and its order and strength holds a significant and unique place even among her most famous contemporaries.

3. To present a text which would find its most valid application in meditation, prayer, and devotion (as I think Julian would have wanted it used), rather than in academic analysis.

Some have attempted the first and lost the woman herself in the process; some have attempted the second and settled for shadows and painful inaccuracy; I know of very few who have intentionally undertaken the third. It is hoped that this work achieves all three of these goals. My personal daily immersion in Julian's character for almost a decade has given me a sympathetic and respectful familiarity (I suspect I would recognize Julian on the street if I were to see her, and I *know* I would recognize her voice!); a theological and linguistic background has provided me with tools for my goal of accuracy; and a life commitment to contemplative prayer has sensitized me, I think, to the devotional dimensions and applications of Julian's work.

This translation is based on one of the three existing manuscripts of the "Long Version" of Julian's book—specifically, British Museum, Sloane Manuscript No. 2499. I am immeasurably indebted to Marion Glasscoe of Exeter University, the editor of the splendid working text of the manuscript whch served as the basis for this translation,[2] and I refer the reader to the introduction to that text for textual vagaries and details, including the opinion that this manuscript probably represents the oldest textual tradition available to us today. In translating, I have also had frequent recourse to the "Paris" manuscript[3] in the working edition of Colledge and Walsh[4] for enrichment, emendations, and textual clarifications. In only a few instances has material from other manuscripts of the work been relied on.[5]

In my effort to retain Julian's style and character in the translation, I have been guided by these principles:

1. I have used obsolete pronoun and verb forms in all forms of direct address, following the pattern of the translators of the Revised Standard Version of the Holy Bible.
2. Where it does not obscure meaning, I have retained some obsolete sentence structure and some forms presently considered to be "ungrammatical."
3. I have left some obsolete words untranslated (e.g. *love-longing, dearworthy, one-ing, well and woe,* etc.) when their sense is relatively clear and exhaustive translation difficult or awkward.
4. I made a difficult decision to retain Julian's own pronouns, even when they are generic and non-gender-specific. Julian's choice intentionally to *mix* gender and sex (e.g., "Christ our Mother, He . . ." or "A man or woman, he . . .") is, I think, of particular value. Further, this is an historical document and there is both an ethical and aesthetic responsibility to be true to it.

217

5. I have omitted all footnotes regarding textual editing, emendation, sources, or expert validations of translations. This decision to omit footnotes does not indicate the absence of serious research, however, and full textual notes will be available in a scholarly edition to be published in the near future.

In my effort to present Julian's ideas and spirituality accurately, I have undertaken the following:

1. Most obvious is the "sense line" arrangement of the text on the page, which is intended to support the meaning, set off tangential, explanatory, and elaborative comments from the on-going body of text, and display clearly the multiple literary parallels so common in Julian's writing.
2. I have translated most technical and theological words which Julian would have known, but which would probably be obscure to most modern readers who lack a classical theological or philosophical education (e.g. *substance* to *essence*).

The "labyrinth of paradox" and the "pyramid of dependent clauses" in Julian's *Revelations* could scarcely be more complicated if the book were in a totally foreign language. Indeed, the task of translation is often compounded, rather than aided, by the common English base the text shares with our modern language.

This can be seen in the work of some of the most highly acclaimed academic translators whose expertise and experience has not protected them from that ever-present and often "invisible" predator— the false cognate.

(One would think that the word *may* was the word *may*, but it isn't—it is a form of the Middle English *mowe* which means "to be able, or have power to." One would think that the word *can* was the word *can*, but it might not be—it could be a form of the Middle English word *canne* which means "to know or understand." And the simple, straightforward clause ". . . althowe synne is not ever the cause . . ." seems to mean what it says, while, in fact, it means almost the opposite when one realizes that the Middle English *ever* is the modern *always*.)

My eye and ear have always been tuned for the relatively intelligent reader who seriously wishes to "pray" this book. My test has been: "Can this lead to insight useful in prayer and will it encourage spiritual growth?" If you share that commitment, if you count yourself among those whom Julian's scribe calls "them that will be His faithful lovers," I welcome you to these pages.

And I add, finally, my best love and gratitude to my Sister Scholastica and my Brother Keith of the Order of Julian of Norwich, who maintained the foundation while I did the building, and gave unstintingly of their own labor and love to bring this to birth.

John-Julian, O.J.N.
Norwich, Connecticut
1987

---

1. Blanchot, Maurice (Davis, Lydia, tr.); *Gaze of Orpheus;* Station Hill.
2. Glasscoe, Marion, ed.; *Julian of Norwich: A Revelation of Love;* Exeter; University of Exeter; 1976.
3. Paris Bibliothèque Nationale Fond anglais 40.
4. Colledge, Edmund & James Walsh, eds.; *A Book of Showings To The Anchoress Julian of Norwich;* Toronto; Pontifical Institute of Mediæval Studies; 1978.
5. Notably: British Museum, Sloane 3705; Upholland Seminary Library; and Westminster Diocesan Archives.
